RISING *with* RESILIENCE

COMPILED BY
Cathy L. Davis

& Dr. Karen Scaglione
DNP, APRN, AGACNP-BC, ACNP-BC

Rising with Resilience
Inspirational Stories Through the Eyes of Medical Professionals, Front-line Workers, Survivors, and the Families and Friends of Those We Miss
UpsiDaisy Press

Published by **UpsiDaisy Press**, St. Louis, MO
Copyright ©2022
All rights reserved.

All contributing authors to this anthology have submitted their chapters to an editing process, and have accepted the recommendations of the editors at their own discretion. All authors have approved their chapters prior to publication.

Cover, Interior Design, and Project Management:
 Davis Creative Publishing Partners, CreativePublishingPartners.com

Compilation by Cathy L. Davis with Dr. Karen Scaglione

Library of Congress Cataloging-in-Publication Data

Library of Congress Control Number: 2022906768

 1. OCC019000   BODY, MIND & SPIRIT / Inspiration & Personal Growth
  2. SELF-HELP / Personal Growth / General   3. MED000000   MEDICAL / General

Rising with Resilience: Inspirational Stories Through the Eyes of Medical Professionals, Front-line Workers, Survivors, and the Families and Friends of Those We Miss

ISBN: 978-1-7347971-9-0 (paperback)
  979-8-9863157-0-6 (ebook)

Dedication

This book is dedicated to my amazing parents who showed me what resilience was,

To my precious mini-me who I hope one day will set trails a blazing while reaching for the stars, and drawing from her own resilience,

To my beautiful friend C.Y. for being my rock always.

To all the medical professionals and front-line workers who tirelessly and compassionately risk their lives to take care of the world.

And to ALL the patients who lost their lives to this pandemic... It was YOU who taught me how to Rise with Resilience in my darkest days as a provider. I will forever be grateful and saddened....
"If I had only had a magic wand"...

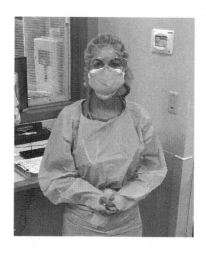

Acknowledgments

My deepest heartfelt thanks to Cathy Davis and her Publishing company for making this book come to life.

Cathy, Jack, Julie, Mary, Rebecca, and Maureen … THANK YOU … THANK YOU for your continuous guidance, patience, and kindness through this entire process…

YOU ARE ALL AMAZING!

TABLE OF CONTENTS

■

**Dr. Karen Scaglione, DNP, APRN,
AGACNP-BC, ACNP-BC, CLNC**

Imbattuto

FASHION, FASHION, FASHION! Pictures of fashion models plastered on my walls; a closet stacked with shoes and dresses, mostly bought after my summer jobs had ended; and my favorite red lipstick always in my backpack. As you can probably guess, I was dumbfounded when my mother came to me as I was entering my first year of college and showed me a paper-made book with my handprint from second grade that said, in bold letters, "WHEN I GROW UP, I WANT TO BE A NURSE."

I looked at her and said, "WHAT?? Seriously, Mom, I am on the fashion track!"

She laughed. "We shall see, Karen."

Without realizing, my medicine spark ignited when I was away at school. I took a detour class called "Science of the Body," because I had to fill my class load. I chose the course because the counselor told me it was an interesting class. I told her, "I like putting clothes on bodies, not dissecting them." She laughed and told me I would enjoy it. I trusted her because she wore the name tag: "Counselor."

I returned home from school early and worked with the medical staff that helped take care of my father who had just been diagnosed with metastatic prostate cancer. That is when my true inspiration for medicine unfolded. I enrolled in the nursing program at Saint Louis University School of Nursing. SURPRISED!? My family wasn't. And I wasn't either.

Graduation day was bittersweet for me. The seat next to my mother was empty. My father passed away six months into my nursing program, but I knew he was looking down from the heavens, beaming, watching me walk across the stage. I have since gone on to finish my masters in nursing, acute care nurse practitioner, and doctoral degrees.

Looking back…. I had the privilege of taking care of my father. Most people do not get that opportunity. I cried daily at the thought of him dying. It was hard to imagine losing such a strong presence in my life. At times, I felt like I failed him because I could not save him. The "rock" was gone. I now cherish all those stern talks, growing and run-like-hell moments knowing I had just pissed him off. I was blessed to have him as a father!

■ ■ ■ ■ ■

I still have a passion for fashion... HA! But nothing compares to practicing medicine. Medicine is amazing! It is the only field that you are accepted into people's lives on a daily basis when they are at their most vulnerable. It is a field that rises above all. Patients and families become one, while embracing each other when the sky darkens. There is a beautiful harmony in medicine that is ever-evolving. I have had the wonderful honor of helping people feel healthier, educating and guiding them to live their best lives, as well as being at the bedside during their final hours on this earth. The latter makes me feel tremendously grateful.

Understanding the conundrums of medicine has made me a stronger provider. Yet, in medicine we are held to a veil of perfection. I will speak for myself and probably many others when I say…I am not perfect and please give me grace when I fall, when I am stressed out, or maybe just a few simple words, "Thank you for all that you do."

What I have truly come to see while taking care of my patients is the bigger picture. It's not just about diagnosing, prescribing medications, and treating the patient; it's stepping away from what you think the patient needs and, instead, hearing their concerns, sitting down and giving the patient the attention they deserve. Practicing medicine is an honor. One working within the field should own it.

I have never wavered regarding my career choice. Admittedly, there have been struggles. The worst was not until early 2020. Boy, did medicine have a curve ball thrown at it via a global pandemic! I know for the many watching the news and reading the articles, it was scary. But it was us, the people in medicine, who came to the table when the world called. We risked our lives and our families' lives to dig deep into the trenches and pull everyone out.

Life right now, practicing medicine, feels like a song lyric: "Why are we here right now and where do we go and why is it so damn hard?" There have been many moments in the past two years that I have thought to myself, *How did this get so out of hand? Maybe I will leave medicine and open a coffee shop. Opening a coffee shop would be a delightful experience compared to the intensive care unit (ICU). Who doesn't like coffee?!*

At the start of the pandemic, I became sick, was presumed positive for the virus and was told to quarantine. My daughter, who was six at the time, had been sick ten days prior, as well as her father. I had just exited my marriage and started divorce proceedings. The stress level was high and the only thought in my head was *You need to stay alive for your child!* No way in hell was I going to die from this virus! Recovery was about a four-week process for me. I struggled with memory, stamina, and smell/taste. When standing in the ICU watching patients suffer from the virus, I had a mixed bag of emotions. I was so grateful to be alive and yet felt terribly saddened for these people that were dying from the same virus.

The daily death toll during the pandemic broke me and my colleagues. In all my years in emergency medicine and critical care, I had never seen so many people die on a daily basis. Every day felt like an invisible enemy attacking from all sides. Patients that appeared to have mild symptoms and talking happily upon admission to the hospital would die in the next twenty-four to forty-eight hours. It shook me to my core to have spoken to these patients, even laughed with them, then to have to call their families in the middle of the night to tell them that their loved one was being placed on a ventilator and they needed to say all their goodbyes. It was that final hour you let the patient ride the "BiPAP wave" to buy them time, hoping you would not have to intubate them to allow them to breath. At times, for reasons I do not know, most ended dying.

I looked at my colleague one day with tears in my eyes and said, "What the hell is going on in this world? How are we going to save all these people!" He looked at me (this stoic figure) with tears in his eyes and said, "Karen, we are not. That's impossible," as he walked away.

I felt shattered after many shifts. My confidence took a hit. Truth be told, at the start of the pandemic, I, as well as many of my colleagues, was terrified of going into rooms of patients with the virus. I had NEVER felt that awful feeling before in my entire career. For us who practice acute care, our mentality is to jump in and run with it. So when I was scared, I felt defeated. I could only imagine the terrifying journey these patients must have been going through. Patients' families were not allowed at the bedside. This brought on many distraught emotions. My mind would trail back to when my father was sick and my just being at the bedside meant so much to him. My heart was crying for these families that could not be with their loved ones.

Entering the ICU corridors became too overwhelming. Now with the hospitalist team, the wreckage is still there, just not as critical. If I had a "magic wand," I would have saved every last soul from this virus! I have a deep sadness for all the lives lost and damaged from this pandemic. The pandemic left wounds and life-long devastation behind. I hope with the latter, will come a soulful healing for all, including myself. God only knows...this world needs it!

As I reflect at this time, I see myself as a woman who has been broken, yet RISEN through the difficulty with inspiration all around me. My years in medicine, and these last eighteen months, have made me resilient and given me a renewed passion for life and medicine. The Lord has blessed me with a priceless career, and it's been one heck of a joyride.

Remember: As you report to each shift, you are much braver and stronger than you believe and much smarter than you realize. I believe ALL of us in medicine are resilient and resourceful, compassionate and caring. We will RISE WITH RESILIENCE as one united community—and make a difference in the lives of those we touch. WE ARE UNDE-FEATED (*Imbattuto*)!

Dr. Karen Scaglione, DNP, APRN, AGACNP-BC, ACNP-BC, CLNC, is an assistant teaching professor at Saint Louis University and an adult geriatric acute care nurse practitioner specializing in emergency and hospitalist medicine. She is the author of "Game Changer: Adult Geriatric Acute Care Nurse Practitioner Fellowship," published in the *Journal of Doctoral Nursing Practice*. She co-authored the manuscript, "Race-Based Trauma Training," as well as a best-selling anthology, *G.R.I.T.*

Karen is CEO of KVinmedical, an independent contracting company, a reviewer for medical legal cases, and is involved in many committees. She currently serves as a content expert in Washington, DC, at the American Nurses Credentialing Center for the national AGACNP exam.

Karen was honored in 2019 by March of Dimes as "Nurse Practitioner of the Year" across Missouri and Illinois. She volunteers in community organizations, such as Adoption/Foster Care Coalition, Nurses for Newborns, and local animal shelters.

Karenscaglione@yahoo.com

■

Nikki Lemley

Magic of The Mundane

It was March 2020 and my son, Jacob, and I drove from St. Louis, Missouri to Dillan, Colorado, to ski during his spring break. We arrived late afternoon, squeezed in a ski run, and then met up with my sister, Ingrid, who lives in Denver, Colorado, and drove up the mountains to join us. We spent a lovely evening with Ingrid and her daughters, Emily, and Grace, catching up and enjoying each other's company. The next morning, we woke up to a ghost town – everything was closed, and people were quarantined. The life-transforming pandemic that would impact our lives in ways we could never imagine had begun.

The fear of infecting someone, or contracting the virus from someone, compounded with the loss of friends and family we love, has created an internal tension for many. It seems insurmountable at times. And for those extroverts, like me, who had to avoid social contact, yet it helps us thrive when engaging with others, has taken its toll! I feel part of me has been temporarily lost. As we attempt to relieve this tension, people are rising with resilience, creating new avenues to fulfill this innate need, and maintain meaningful relationships.

The silver lining of COVID has been that we have turned to creativity and innovation to navigate these very murky and perplexing waters. In 2021, as President of the Webster Groves/Shrewsbury/Rock Hill Chamber of Commerce, I was given the honor to virtually recognize recipients of our "Creativity in Crisis" awards where our local businesses, organizations and even students were nominated for their contributions during this tumultuous time. Witnessing pivotal changes in businesses and acts of compassion and kindness by our community members uplifted all of us and provided a window for celebration.

Being confined within our homes has triggered many emotions—gratitude in being able to spend more time with family (including the furry ones) and frustration in having to ensure our children are still learning through a computer screen. On top of that, loneliness and isolation has added yet more stress to an already untenable situation, with no real solution or end. Many of us have experienced this entire range of feelings and, for me, letting these emotions percolate has forged new perspectives of what is important.

As a mother of sixteen-year-old twins when the pandemic began, chance encounters became more frequent, and these moments became the highlight of my day—at least most days. Having a spontaneous discussion in the kitchen or just being available to bounce an idea off me and their dad has been a pleasure I never expected. It has brought to my attention that the daily, mundane moments you experience can be the most impactful. When reflecting on your life, while the big events and celebrations are important milestones, the subtleties of everyday engagement, touching base and being available are the times that build relationships and trust with each other. These are the moments that fill us with the emotional nourishment that helps to sustain us during the more tumultuous times we will encounter.

There are some relationships you get to select and others, due to work and family connections, you do not. We each get to make a conscious choice in how to engage in these relationships. Dr. Marlowe Erickson, a friend and psychiatrist who has passed away, would say we have a choice to put our hand on the hot stove or not. In other words, we get to choose whether we want to feel negativity or not. In my role as a health insurance broker, I am able to educate people so they can make informed decisions that will protect them. I also spend a great deal of time on the phone having to select from prompts that do not align with the information I am seeking and long hold times that may or may not result in the information I need. During these times, I am reminded of Marlowe's message of deciding whether or not I will remove my hand from the stove. This reminder leads to other creative endeavors such as multi-tasking while on hold to lessen my checklist for the day. All of us experience these moments and they have been exacerbated due to the pandemic. Remembering that we can take a breath and make an informed choice can change your day from not so good to great.

Victor Frankl, a holocaust survivor, and author of Man's Search for Meaning, wrote, "Between stimulus and response there is a space. In that space is our power to choose our response. In our response lies our growth and our freedom." My mentor, Glenn Detrick, taught a class at Washington University in St. Louis and this was one of his required books. Despite the horrors Dr. Frankl encountered, he maintained his free will in choosing his reaction. This knowledge is a gift I give myself daily with humility and extreme gratitude. Through this lens, I am better equipped to rise with resilience, despite the circumstances.

In December 1994, my husband, Tom, and I were married. One month later, we arrived in Ukraine with the fourth US Peace Corps group and served from January 1995 - March 1997. Our group was comprised mostly of newly minted MBAs and retired CEOs, and we were there to help stimulate a market economy after the collapse of the former Soviet Union in 1991. After our three months of language and culture training in Lutzk, we moved to Lviv, Ukraine where I consulted at the Lviv Institute of Management and taught business English. Tom worked in City Hall where he worked with PADCO, Planning & Development Collaborative International, Inc., a contractor with USAID (United States Agency for International Development) to assist with developing a better infrastructure for water in the city. People living in Lviv were limited to having water and electricity during specific times of the day and the periods of time with no access were referred to as "brown outs." Without electricity, we were grateful for gas stoves and actually looked forward to our candle-light dinners.

After Peace Corps, we continued to live and work in Kyiv, Ukraine for an additional five years. I was the Human Resource Manager for Western Newly Independent States Enterprise Fund (WNISEP) and we invested in Ukrainian businesses, providing the resources they needed to be profitable. Tom consulted with different US contractors in Ukraine. We absolutely loved the time we spent in Ukraine and learned a great deal about Ukraine and the people who live there, as well as about ourselves. I love the fact that Tom affectionately refers to our time in Ukraine as our eight-year honeymoon.

On a Sunday in June 2002, after spending the weekend in Crimea, we were heading back to Kyiv on a small plane "puddle jumper" and noticed that people were elbowing their way to get to the plane entrance. We had tickets and did not understand what was going on. When we made it to the entrance, we learned that they had sold more tickets than seats and we were not going to make it home. Other prospective passengers in our situation began arguing and insisted that we be allowed aboard. We were given the option of riding in the cargo hold with no temperature control or seat belts or staying in Crimea. We joined a group of six other people and made our way back to Kyiv in this most unsafe and unusual manner. In hindsight it was definitely not the most responsible decision, but it was certainly an adventure and was one among many in the culture we fondly referred to as "The Wild East."

We chose Ukraine instead of Poland as our Peace Corps destination because neither of us had ever heard of it. Needless to say, we entered a culture unlike anything we had ever experienced. Initially, we questioned the silence and furtive looks people gave us in public. We came to learn that we were viewed as spies – why else would Americans come to Ukraine? As we began developing friendships through our work and were invited to our colleagues' homes, we experienced hospitality in a way we could never have imagined. They had so little, yet we were treated like royalty, and we were honored to hear their stories behind closed doors. We developed close friendships and are still friends with quite a few of the people we worked with. The invasion of Ukraine has been heartbreaking for us and the entire world, but Ukrainians have risen with resilience generation after generation, and I am optimistic that they will do so again.

Never before have relationships been so important to me. I have learned that when fear and despair seem to pierce our humanity, being present and savoring the everyday, mundane exchanges with much more appreciation and gratitude pave a much richer, more optimistic, and generous path.

Nikki is a health insurance broker and enjoys being able to educate and advise individuals and businesses as they navigate their way through this complex and ever-changing industry. Nikki holds a BSBA in Business Administration from the University of Maryland, a Master's Certificate in International Affairs from Washington University, and an Executive MBA (EMBA) from Washington University's Olin Business School. Nikki is also a graduate of the Art & Science of Coaching through Erickson College, based in Canada.

Nikki is the proud mother of eighteen-year-old twins, Margo and Jacob, and is married to Tom, a Social Security Disability attorney. They have lived in Webster Groves, Missouri for the past 15 years.

Nikki is a community leader and loves to travel, spend time in nature, and experience life with family and friends. Nikki lived abroad cumulatively for fourteen years in Germany, Ukraine, and Azerbaijan.

nikkilemley@gmail.com
www.linkedin.com/in/nikkilemley/
www.facebook.com/nikki.lemley.5

■

Heather Wade, DNP, FNP-BC, RN

Small Ripples Eventually Make Big Waves

Florence Nightingale, a nurse in the 1800s, wrote an oath that nursing students still recite today upon graduation from nursing school. The oath, in conjunction with a modern-day code of ethics, reminds nurses that kindness, compassion, integrity, pragmatism, fidelity, and veracity are vital qualities of a nurse. Never have these characteristics mattered more than during a relentless pandemic.

RISING UP as a nurse during the pandemic, I had to remember these foundational characteristics of my call to nursing. Throughout the pandemic, I worked both as a public health nurse educator and a primary care family nurse practitioner. Many days, I had to keep both myself and my students going because we had unabating work to do in a timeline that mattered. Despite exhaustion, we together maintained fidelity—a faithfulness to professional promises and the provision of safe and high-quality care in a compassionate manner.

In the age of misinformation and social media, another segment of my oath as a nurse is to exhibit veracity. A nurse must be completely truthful to patients and not hide the whole truth, even if this may lead to patient distress. I had hundreds of conversations related to vaccine safety and efficacy as well as the risk of natural immunity versus immune boosted immunity. Sometimes these are hard conversations, but they are rooted in truth and encompass both fidelity and veracity.

It is absolutely overwhelming to be a public health nurse in a pandemic. I was able to work in an upstream prevention role directing mass vaccination and testing clinics for my city and university. My niche, my groove, is here in my community as a source of evidence-based information and truth. As guidelines changed seemingly every 48 hours, it was my job to keep up with them, educate my students, and then execute a mass vaccination clinic the next day.

On a personal level, colleagues, friends, and family reached out frequently, wondering what guideline applied to them, how to start their quarantine count and manage symptoms, recommendations for the best mask for traveling, and where to find the ever-elusive rapid antigen test. My brain felt like it was in overdrive, and I didn't feel like I was doing any job well. Therefore, I learned to focus on making a difference for one person at a time. *Small ripples make big waves of change.*

To date, I have personally given thousands of vaccines. In the winter of 2021, when we were rolling out the initial wave of vaccines, there was such a buzz of hope! It was empowering! There was an event in downtown St. Louis, MO where we were vaccinating first responders. It was awesome to thank them for their service and know we were working mutually to keep our community safe. It felt like we were all in it together, and everyone had an important role to play. I teach my students that in public health, the community is our patient. This was well modeled for them while vaccinating first responders!

There was also a moment during one of those early clinics when a pregnant woman came through the line for her vaccine. Her immense gratitude brought her to tears. She thanked me for taking care of her and her baby. I am an easy crier, and this definitely brought me to tears. That same day, one of my nursing students was also able to personally vaccinate his own elderly grandmother. She effusively thanked him for learning to be a nurse and for protecting her. The tears continued to flow.

Another weekend, my students and I set up a clinic in a church basement to provide vaccines for parishioners who were participating in drive through communion (church attendance was still limited at this time.) We called this event *'The Bread, The Body, and The Booster'*; it had a nice ring to it!

Throughout the spring of 2021, I continued to find myself at a variety of vaccine clinics, and I had lists of people to text when I had extras. I would go from home to home with my vaccine, my sharps container, and my emergency kit. I started to call it *Moderna Door Dash*! I also recognized that I have an odd love of language. Some people bring chocolates or words of affirmation; I bring needles!

Virus testing also provided an opportunity for many vignettes. Guess what happens when it's winter in St. Louis, the temperature is 12 degrees, and you're performing drive up testing outside? What happens is that your gloves freeze and break! It was difficult to perform a nasal swab with broken gloves and frozen fingers. I just had to laugh and continue to pivot as a bad attitude will get me nowhere! The more known positive cases, the less community spread. Each prevented case is someone's loved one that remains healthy. *Small ripples make big waves of change.*

RISING UP as an educator of the next generation of nurses has felt all consuming and overwhelming. Mentoring the next generation of nurses has never felt so applicable or necessary. We need these new nurses to be *really good* and *really ready* to go as soon as they graduate.

I think it's important to realize that in addition to the sickness and death these young graduates bear witness to, they also see headlines of nurses leaving in droves, nurses working obscene hours, and nurses' safety impeded with a lack of protective equipment. How can you inspire new generations despite toxic headlines and difficult patient care? I decided to do small and subtle encouragements by incorporating inspirational nursing stories into every lecture, in hopes of providing a bigger picture of all that a nurse *can do*! I also provide a lot of space for them to debrief death witnessed.

Another difficulty of being a nurse educator in the time of a pandemic is searching for the elusive balance of maintaining rigor while also providing emotional support to the students. These newly graduated nurses will be caring for the patients who have worsened chronic illnesses because of extended time without access to providers. At the same time, these students were struggling with common pandemic woes: limited social interaction, missing class while on quarantine, and feeling the angst of living in an unprecedented time. To guide my moral compass and plans for teaching, I thought back to Florence Nightingale and her oath to fidelity and veracity. Ultimately, I maintained the difficulty of my exams and the expectations of clinical outcomes to ensure the provision of safe and high-quality care in a compassionate manner, while I tried to balance student distress. At the time of this writing, we are still in the midst of educating nurses during a pandemic and sending them out to the wild west. I haven't had the time and space to reflect about whether the maintenance of rigor was the right teaching method, but I have still witnessed students having a 'lightbulb' breakthrough moment and building deep connection with patients. I do genuinely hope this will inspire RISING in my students!

The health of my patients and the success and empowerment of my students are primary. I could not *Rise Up* without remembering my steady baseline of fidelity and veracity with a healthy dose of flexibility. These are all qualities I want to instill in my students and subsequently, allow my children to witness.

RISING UP as a human, a wife, and a mother has been more difficult than *RISING UP* as a professional. The hard and heavy work relates to our core, our faith, our parenting, and our personal relationships. Despite disappointment, we can look for joy. Joy and gratitude feed my resilience. There are many gratitude practices I employ. I look for silver linings, enjoy simple pleasures, and celebrate small victories. When I look for where God is meeting me, I realize that the pandemic has only enhanced my parenting goals. I want to raise healthy, happy, well-adjusted kids who have a faith and grit. I want them to serve others. I want them to be generous. Because of the pandemic, I know where they thrive and where they struggle. I know how they learn and how they are academically motivated. The gift of learning about my children will never be time wasted.

My husband and I get to highlight the common good and how our mask wearing, social distancing, and social sacrifices are about the common good. Additionally, the kids have watched a healthy partnership ebb and flow. In 2021, I worked 21 weekends. My husband managed the family on top of his own full-time job without ever grumbling. Contributions to the pandemic come in all shapes and sizes. Healthy partnerships contribute to resilience.

In the end, productive resilience for me, as a human, looks like focusing on what I *can do* and knowing that small actions culminate into ripples of change. I have structured my career choices around helping people to receive care and tried not to focus on those who could access care but are unwilling. I have thoroughly read the evidence-based practice surrounding vaccines so that I can practice and teach fidelity and veracity. These are small things that I *can do* that are in my wheelhouse. I can embrace that my varied roles culminate to do good work for such a time as this. I can sow hope, I can care for others, and I can press forward, one day at a time.

Heather Wade DNP, FNP-BC, RN has been a registered nurse for 17 years and a doctorally-prepared family nurse practitioner for 11 years. She is currently in a full-time nursing faculty role at Saint Louis University, and she also spends time each week providing primary and public health care as a nurse practitioner in the community. Heather is married to Mike, and they are parents to three incredible kids aged 11, 9, and 7 who have naturally endured virtual learning, sports with masks, and limited inside play dates for two years. The children have risen up with a grace, hope, and positivity that is beyond inspirational. As a family they are trying to visit all 50 states, and they love exploring national parks.

www.facebook.com/heather.c.wade

■

L. Carol Scott, PhD

Rising On Purpose

The advent of the pandemic in the U.S. stole the gas out of my tank, ripped the miles off my tires, and slowed my journey. That is a literal statement as well as a metaphor. The worldwide virus stopped me in my tracks in more ways than one.

For all of 2019 and the first two months of 2020, I was an itinerant author and speaker, traveling the lower 48 states of this amazing country as I clarified my brand and built my audience. Buying an RV in September 2018 and selling my sticks-and-bricks house in November committed me to a full-time life on the road, which I officially began as I drove out of St. Louis on January 8, 2019. From that start, through January 7, 2020, I traveled 19,191 miles through 40 states in the little RV I call She Who.

I shared my tiny home on wheels with a mid-sized senior dog I named Journey, adopted from a Chattanooga shelter on January 18th after my first speaking engagement. Across those 12 months, I spoke on messages from my first book, *Just Be Your S.E.L.F.—Your Guide to Improving Any Relationship*, and wrote a second one. I released *Let the Child Shine: Teaching to the Brilliance in a Young Child* at a November 2019 national conference, one of the last of my 14 speaking venues of this year on the road.

As we traveled, the idea that I might find a new place to settle morphed into a desire to continue as a full-time RV nomad. And so, in January 2020, Journey, She Who, and I rolled out of Portland, Oregon into a second year, following the road to more speaking engagements, until we landed in Tucson on March 1ˢᵗ. A short visit with local friends to enjoy the lovely weather meant we were still there for the national declaration of a pandemic on March 13ᵗʰ, and we hunkered down in one place for an unprecedented 16 weeks. No more rolling. No more speaking.

And I started to get scared. Not just scared of catching the virus—or losing loved ones to it, as the numbers of sick and dying climbed and the daily news turned dire—but scared of losing my livelihood. Who hires speakers when there are no public gatherings? At first, almost nobody.

Everywhere, businesses were "pivoting" around the new normal of life at social distance. But my business was barely begun, and I yet lacked an anchor in the speaker industry around which to pivot. Staying in one place, with no work, I felt more adrift than I had in 14 months of travel.

I began fretfully focusing on how to earn an income, rather than on building what I saw as a life purpose into a brand and gathering its audience. And that mental shift added emotional and spiritual forms of "stuckness" to the physical hunkering. As I lost my literal road ahead, my sense of my place in the world began to fade as well. Like Dorothy's dream of the Land of Oz, my rolling life "on purpose" seemed to fade into a barely remembered haze.

My version of the pandemic wasn't the nightmare endured by many others. My new life was eased in many ways. A far-away friend mailed me some homemade masks and the RV park extended my rental agreement indefinitely. I adapted quickly to the new routines of online shopping, with deliveries or furtive parking lot pick-ups. My social contacts were mostly limited to six feet of separation from those delivery workers and the office staff at the RV park. I did have occasional visits from one of the local friends in my "bubble," while the other was too at-risk for even the most protected of contact. My biggest struggle was finding decent toilet paper to be delivered.

Physically, I was safe. In all the other aspects of self, my health deteriorated quickly. I angrily focused on the small-minded thinking of national "leaders" whose decisions and messages worsened the pandemic's ravages. This woman courageously driven by faith in a purpose collapsed into one quivering in fear. And my fear and anger weren't just about the pandemic. I watched the balance in my retirement account shrinking as each month's expenses passed without offsetting income. I began to fear an impoverished future, furiously blaming the administration's fumbling of our nation's response to this worldwide problem.

The heat of Tucson's summer finally prompted me into a short, terrified trip up to the mountains of southern Colorado. Eight weeks near Mesa Verde followed by four weeks in Santa Fe led me back south to Albuquerque. This stopover was planned for two nights on my way to Mexico for the winter and had long been a pin in my map for an annual check-up with a cardiologist, assessing the status of a diagnosis I'd been managing for 15 years.

The doc's news was not good for me, and Journey's vet check in Santa Fe had resulted in worse news – a very short life expectancy for my canine companion. Thoroughly disheartened by now, I felt as physically vulnerable as I was emotionally, mentally, and spiritually. Despite the phenomenal lift by many beloveds—via supportive messages as well as hard cash to a GoFundMe effort—I still felt alone and finally, utterly bereft of inner strength.

Moving through the loss of dog-girl Journey, adding yet another journey through diagnostic testing and changes in medications, and living through eight more months of little income and many expenses completed my transformation into what I now can see was a former version of myself. Off-center, flailing in fear and self-doubt, nearly out of funds, and worried about what was to come, I finally left Albuquerque at the end of May 2021 and began a long journey back to Portland Oregon, via a not-at-all-on-the-way family reunion in Kansas City, MO.

And then, in mid-July of 2021, settled beside the Columbia River for a month, I began to rise from the prostration in which I found myself. I reconnected to my chosen faith practice through a fortuitously timed class titled *Building a Healing Consciousness* and began to reconstruct my pre-pandemic consciousness. I found the anchor I needed, around which to pivot. Not my business, yet, but—much more importantly—my life.

In the final session of the six-week class, I joined remotely from my next stop in the Bay Area, parked in the driveway of my godson. I was joined by his mom—my bestie of 50 years—to briefly share the care of her grandchildren, who are also my "great godkids," while their folks took a vacation.

Always balm for my soul, this friend and I share lessons and learning in the twin realms of spiritual and personal development. We lift each other, teach each other, and challenge each other with mutual trust, respect, and love. Spending a couple of weeks with two preschoolers was equally nourishing for my heart and soul, as I continued to relocate my conscious center, my heart, and my purpose.

Onward and upward, I rose. The fear and worry of the prior 18 months began to fall away like an old carapace that no longer fit the thrumming, renewing cicada within. The rising wasn't so much like flying, but more like climbing a tree trunk faster and more nimbly, having released my tether to some unseen hold, below.

With no reasonable expectation of income to cover the expense, I intuitively followed an opportunity, committing to six months of applied neurology coaching. That work to heal my Vagus nerve system, wired by seven of the 10 Adverse Childhood Experiences (ACEs),[1] was utterly life changing. And so, I rose ever faster and higher, as I followed my earlier plan to over-winter in Mexico. I first spent a month in San Diego to establish a new "medical home," and then rolled on to Ensenada in Baja, where I would "moochdock" with family.

By then, completely out of my nest egg and relying on Social Security for my primary income, I still chose to embrace yet another extra expense. Tuning my remote connection back to my Portland spiritual home, I enrolled in a class on the origins of my faith philosophy: the course they call "The Roots" of our shared beliefs.

1 See www.lcarolscott.com/face-your-aces for more information

And BAM! The tree trunk didn't change. My speed and agility to climb remained about the same. But now the base of that tree was re-connected to deep and stable roots. Suddenly, as before the pandemic's fear pulled my focus, I could clearly see all the negative thoughts and feelings, draped like wet towels in need of a wash, above me and below. Upon them, my feet and hands had been slipping and losing grip. Now they were falling from my path, as if pulled away by a thousand invisible hands. And so it was; so they were.

Rising with Resilience in the pandemic has, for me, meant relocating familiar and comforting tools I seemed to lose in its early months. They were, I believe, never really lost, but I had allowed myself to be distracted from their abundant presence. I began to believe in the negative images and messages of the media, always ready for consumption, always waiting to fill my heart with darkness and foreboding. I allowed my eyes and ears to be pulled away from what I *know* to be the truth—the Truth—of my path.

Throughout my life, *rising* has always been enabled by that truth, that certain knowledge of a center and a purpose that no external circumstances can touch. It has been about knowing I have an ever-present path, which carries infinite power, and is always wise in guiding each foot to where it should go next…and next…and next…

Like surviving seven ACEs, like continuing to recover from brain-wiring trauma, like forging 35 years of sobriety, like building a new business…*resilience*, for me, is about staying on path, on purpose. It's about returning over and over to that brilliantly lighted, guided path, whenever I am led away by fear of the unknown, or by twinkling fairy lights that look like relief from the dark, or by any other influence that compels me to stray.

The way is always present. I simply need to remind my wandering awareness to find it again. *For me, that life on purpose is the path of resilience. That path is what enables me, always, to rise again.*

Dr. L. Carol Scott is a trauma-informed developmental psychologist, TEDx speaker, coach, and author. Carol brings the SASS—Self-Aware Success Strategies—to help you get along better on the adult playgrounds where you play.

Carol knows that your success today is determined by your first seven years of life. And she also knows that it's never too late for Development Do-Overs. As her coaching client, you bring your unique goals for success, and she draws out your SASS. Together, you repattern how you operate in the relationships that are at the heart of achievement.

Also a nationally respected thought leader in early care and education (ECE), Carol is former president of the board for Child Care Aware® of America. She is the ECE System Integration Consultant for Steering Impact, the home of EarlyCare+, a technology innovation that revolutionizes access for all parents and caregivers to the ecosystem of ECE services.

carol@lcarolscott.com
www.facebook.com/dr.l.carolscott
www.instagram.com/dr.l.carol
www.linkedin.com/in/dr-l-carol-scott-7b70429/

■

Theresa McTigue, RN, BSN, FNP-C

A Little Bit of Luck

In the spring of 2006, I eagerly ran to the mailbox to find a letter of acceptance to a nursing program that I anticipated would **not have** wanted me.
I was graduating high school, and at the advice of my mother, I applied to
first year entry nursing programs. She said, "you just need a prayer and a
little bit of luck". Looking back, it was probably the best advice I could have
received.

Growing up, I had a feeling of "responsibility" when someone close
to me was ill, injured, or emotionally compromised. I felt the need to stay
close to that person, even just to dry their tears or give a hug. This feeling
throughout my young life is likely what inspired me to consider entering
the medical field.

Fast forward four years to 2010, and I was standing in my cap and
gown. I thought to myself "this might have been a mistake." Considering
I leaned on the shy side of the social spectrum, I was uneasy heading into
job interviews. I did not feel prepared for the "real world" of nursing, nor
did it seem like I had much to offer as far as skill or expertise. In 2010, the
nursing jobs were not as abundant as I had hoped.

Just as I was about to jump into a part time position, the VA hospital
contacted me about a new "residency" program. Anticipating what was
advertised (several months of rotations within different specialty areas
with classroom and educational opportunities), I decided to accept.
Unfortunately, the program did not deliver what was promised, as I was

placed in an outpatient clinic for several months before finally starting full time on a cardiac floor. To say the least, I was disappointed! Yet I jumped in, determined to learn as much as possible. Once that real life, "hands on" learning started, let me tell you, it did not stop!

One specific night stands out in my memory—"hectic" is the only word that describes my shift. As I was running around, cleaning up messes and stabilizing disasters, a clear thought floated through my mind: "this is what I am meant to do." *It nearly stopped me in my tracks!* I had not eaten, gone to the bathroom, or had one second to think since I clocked in at 7:00 p.m. I was not really enjoying the evening; I was stressed, sweaty, and scrambling. Yet this calming thought had come to me, and I finished out the rest of the shift with a little more energy and focus.

Something clicked that night and sent me on an adventure I never saw myself doing. I applied for graduate school. *I knew that medicine had grabbed a hold of me!*

Eventually functioning as a charge nurse, the complex critical thinking and fast pace of it all, brought so much joy! I loved configuring staffing solutions and assisting the whole floor. The mindset, *every patient IS my patient*, was somehow comforting and felt like I was actually making a difference.

Once I started graduate school, the way I looked at patients and their medical records changed. It was a puzzle I wanted to put together: the cause and effect of the events leading up to hospitalization. How could this be prevented? How did one condition lead to another? And on and on. I dug deep through medical records, wanting to know more and more.

A few years later I was, again, standing in a cap and gown. But this time I did not think I had made a mistake. I was excited and extremely proud! I was offered a hospitalist position which would provide me with invaluable initial experience. It was interesting to wrap my mind around the change from bedside nurse to provider. *The one in the white coat.* When I walked into the room, I needed to have a plan. To be ready to explain my rationale, provide evidence, and interpret diagnostics in laymen's terms. This proved challenging but absolutely rewarding. I enjoyed building relationships with physicians, working alongside them as colleagues and teammates. Learning from them was probably the best part of the job.

I continued my path in the hospitalist world, this time taking on a position at a larger, tertiary hospital. The patient population was more complicated, and it almost felt like I was starting over. I learned to juggle a bigger patient load, provide overnight coverage, and admit seriously ill and complex patients. I will be the first to admit that I cried after several of my initial shifts. If working in a hospital does not pull at your heart strings, then you are most likely doing it wrong. *Medicine is a science, but it is also an art: it is emotional, nerve wracking, and adrenaline pumping.* You can go from doing nothing to doing everything in a matter of seconds. It is not for the faint of heart.

I took a short break from my career after having my first child. I was uneasy heading back into work, leaving my new baby behind at home. I considered being a stay-at-home mom. However, I knew I would miss the hubbub and excitement of hospital life. I jumped back in at full pace, just to find out after several months that I was expecting another baby. The exciting news was soon dampened by the start of the pandemic. My son was born two weeks before the world shut down in March 2020. My son was a bit early and required a week-long stay in the special nursery. I left with him in my arms on the day the hospital started restricting visitors. For the first time since starting in medicine, I was relieved to be walking out of a hospital with no intention of returning anytime soon.

Being at home with a newborn at the start of a pandemic was likely one of the most challenging and strangest experiences of my life. I had no visitors. I was petrified to leave my house. Family came to peek at him through the windows but were not allowed inside. We had supplies delivered at the doorstep. We watched daily presidential briefings of impending societal collapse and untimely deaths at a massive scale. This does not bode well for a post-partum mother who is also dealing with "baby blues" and sleep deprivation. Not to mention that I felt some guilt knowing I was safer at home on maternity leave versus my colleagues facing the unknown. My heart goes out to all the new mothers who sat at home alone during that first year. We will not get those experiences back; we lost that opportunity for "normal."

Eventually I returned to work several months into the pandemic. I was lucky enough to jump back in during a "lull." The number of virus cases was down; and research was available for treatment recommendations. I still remember walking into my first virus positive room and feeling absolutely sick to my stomach. Several thoughts floated through my mind: Will I catch it? Will I bring it home to my baby and toddler? What if I make a mistake and this person gets worse? How do they feel being in the hospital alone with no visitors? Will they ever see their family again? Despite all these thoughts, I did the best I could with what information was available.

Time ticked forward and unfortunately another wave took over the hospital. It was around the holidays, and the feeling of "dread" was literally palpable. I lost track one night of how many calls I received about rapidly deteriorating patients. *I felt hopeless.* I cannot imagine what this would have been like before Airvo devices were invented and readily available. This device can deliver high levels of oxygen; and I can only assume it saved many people from ending up on the ventilator.

Unknown at the time, this device would soon be lifesaving for my own family! We all ended up with the virus; my mother suffering the most. She was admitted to the hospital. *I got to experience first-hand how it felt to literally be dragged away from a loved one.* I watched them wheel her into the room and as the nurse pushed me out, I wondered – will I ever see her again?

Lucky for us, the Airvo device and newest treatments worked in her favor. She walked out of the hospital eight days later, weak and on oxygen, but alive. I have never felt so relieved. I did, however, have a new sense of understanding and empathy for patients and their family during the pandemic.

We are now over two years into this mess, and I really do believe it is a crime to cut off visitors in the hospital. I understood it in the beginning when the world was shut down, but as time passed, I think it is wrong for people to be alone, die alone, frightened/scared/gasping for air without a loved one by their side. *Provide PPE and let these people have their family by their sides.*

I hope this pandemic has reminded everyone that life is precious, but it is not guaranteed. I have learned just how quickly a situation can get out of control and how our healthcare system could easily collapse. Although it has been a difficult two years, I have grown into an overall better clinician; with more compassion and patience. I am looking forward to raising my children in a post-pandemic world, whatever that may look like.

Theresa McTigue started her journey in healthcare in 2009. She has worked as a patient care technician, bedside nurse, and nurse practitioner. She received her master's degree in 2015. She has worked in hospitalist medicine since that time. She remains on night shift, which she enjoys, striving to be a calming and constant presence during the often chaotic and understaffed hours of the hospital. As a healthcare provider, she believes in being an active listener, being proactive in her patient's care, and assuring each family member that their loved one is in good hands. She is married with two toddlers and enjoys spending her free time with them.

Theresa McTigue, RN, BSN, FNP-C
theresamctigue@gmail.com

Susan Veenstra

The Healing Power of Music

"Dear Music, thank you for always clearing my head, healing my heart, and lifting my spirits."

-Lori Deschene

Before the pandemic, I had been living with an undiagnosed food allergy that was making me sick, and I did not know it! The adverse effects of this unknown illness affected my daily life; however, my doctors could not determine the cause of my symptoms. I learned to adapt, manage, and function despite the uncertainty—for the most part. Music helped me cope during my journey to wellness.

In 2016, I started a successful music business, teaching students from 6 years of age to senior citizens, offering individual and group lessons on piano, keyboards, organ, as well as voice and musical audition preparation. My students learned to play music in a variety of genres, including classical, pop/rock, blues, jazz, Latin, and religious.

My former teachers were my mentors who helped me establish my thriving music studio. I was warmly welcomed into the Piano Teachers Round Table of St. Louis. One of my proudest moments is recalled in a photo of my April 2019 recital, where I am pictured with a group of students on the stage. My beaming smile reflected so much joy and pride in my students' success and achievements. My business was flourishing and progressing exactly as I had planned. By January 2020, I had grown my studio and doubled the number of students—I was so close to reaching my goal! Unfortunately, in February we heard the foreboding news that the virus was spreading to multiple countries, ours included.

Abruptly in March 2020, our in-person lessons ended when the shocking magnitude of the virus resulted in lockdown and quarantines. Subsequently, this was followed by 14 months of virtual lessons and three (THREE!) virtual recitals. This threw me out of my "comfort zone" and helped me *Rise with Resilience* into the "growth zone" of 100% online lessons, schedule changes, new equipment purchases and installation, rearranging furniture and moving a grand piano, expensive book purchases (teacher copies of all my students' books), more preparation, and creating online payment options. We utilized FaceTime, Skype, and Zoom. In the next months, I lost some beginner students who needed one-on-one attention and could not effectively learn virtually. I also faced the inability to enroll new students in the upcoming months, as well as the next school year. With the loss of current and potential students, my income suffered significantly. Sadly, I would have reached my enrollment goal had it not been for the pandemic.

It was difficult dealing with the range of negative emotions: uncertainty, frustration, sadness, and anger. I turned to the piano to boost my mood. Sometimes, all I needed was to play one or two Chopin pieces and I would feel better. The moment my fingers touched the black and white keys, I could feel the tension drain from my body and the cacophony inside my head would subside. Other times, I reached for one of my "angry songs" and pounded out frustration as the horses raced in Godard's "Le Cavalier Fantastique." The song ended with burning muscles, a huge exhale, and a slump of my shoulders. Physically and mentally, playing the piano is exercise, using many muscles throughout the body. As my mood began to improve, my internal optimist chose a hopeful frame of mind with "Hymne" by Vangelis.

Somehow, I made a necessary mental shift: I chose to rise above by elevating my teaching. I tried to provide normalcy and routine for my students via Zoom lessons. It was important to me to reflect a positive attitude for the kids, demonstrate innovative problem-solving, and show perseverance and resilience despite challenges. As I embraced change and adapted, I found myself entering my "creative zone"! I was passionate, excited, driven, and on a mission! I designed theme weeks, provided activity calendars, suggested learning projects, and sent practice videos. "Porch pickup packets" were available monthly: these included new music, goal sheets, coloring pages, theory worksheets, seasonal stickers, and empowerment exercises ("If I Were in Charge of the World, I Would…" fill in the blank). At the beginning of a lesson, I held up a sign which read "I Miss Your FACE" (F-A-C-E: treble clef space notes). I played carnival games with students to reinforce skills. My students brought JOY and I enjoyed their presence on the screen. We cheered each other up—our mutual enthusiasm was contagious!

In my free time, I immersed myself in art and music, surrounded by family pets. Our animals offered more comfort to me than I ever imagined! I painted on canvas, hand-pieced quilt tops, and cooked new recipes, while listening to podcasts, watching movie musicals and sports game replays. I connected with an online community of musicians, music teachers, makers, and artists. The support from the virtual meeting of creative minds on social media was beneficial to me. My weekly routine included watching our live-stream church service, which we learned to cast from a cell phone to the big screen in our family room. In my neighborhood, I tried to convey upbeat vibes to my community through sidewalk chalk messages and handmade window posters.

My positivity was challenged in January 2021, when I received the news that my mentor, friend, and former teacher passed away. This unexpected loss left me heartbroken. Her family asked me to play the piano for her memorial service. I fought back tears as I played her favorite Chopin piece on the grand piano. It was a small gathering, due to the virus. The pandemic continued with another variant and an unbelievable loss of life, and we were only just gleaning when the vaccine distribution would begin. In April, I was able to be vaccinated as an adult: I felt a huge sense of relief. At that time, children under 18 would not be able to be vaccinated until more research studies were complete. It was not clear when in-person lessons could resume.

Months later, I contracted the virus in December 2021 during the next virus mutation, after being vaccinated and boosted. I was surprised, but then I remembered that the vaccine does not prevent you from getting the virus, it just minimizes symptoms. My symptoms lingered longer than expected. The virus' symptoms, combined with my existing condition, distressed me enough to seek medical treatment. My journey of seeing various doctors led me to an allergist who tested and diagnosed me with a rare food allergy, finally solving my health mystery! She explained how to change my diet and prescribed an Epi-pen for potential anaphylaxis. I learned about Alpha-Gal Syndrome (AGS), which appears to develop after a tick bite and causes an allergic reaction to red (mammalian) meat and by-products, including dairy and gelatin. (This also applies to over-the-counter medicines, drugs and medical treatments containing mammal-derived ingredients.) AGS is a spreading problem with more and more people being diagnosed. I started meeting with an "allergy-informed" counselor to help manage the stress. I reconnected with friends with known food allergies, and they offered helpful resources. This was a huge learning curve. My thoughts feeling crowded, I turned to Beethoven's "Für Elise" and reached a state of mindfulness as I played the beautiful music.

In March 2022, my "silver lining" outcome from the pandemic is that I reached a diagnosis sooner due to having the virus. My online research led me to believe I needed to see a specialist. I had to be my own advocate and pursue getting the answers I needed. (Interestingly, I know two other people who received a health diagnosis because of having the virus.) Having changed my diet, I feel significantly more energetic, healthy, and hopeful! Moving forward with intention, I am doing more writing, traveling, exercising, and focusing on my mental health. I will continue to find peace through my music. The future of AGS research and community awareness is important to me and many others; therefore, I will contribute to this cause as much as I can. In addition, I have a renewed appreciation for the plight of people who have "invisible" illnesses. All of us need to recognize that invisible illnesses bring people down and we do not even realize it. Sometimes testing is inconclusive, and patients must help reach their own diagnosis, as in my case. It can take years to obtain some diagnoses.

This is my story, which I am openly sharing with the hope that I can help and inspire someone who may be suffering mentally and physically. If you are struggling, you must find ways to cope, whatever that means to you. Allow yourself to partake in self-care and delve into a hobby. Explore what is therapeutic for you. P-I-A-N-O spells relief for me. What spells relief for you? Find it. Don't give up on yourself; fight for what you need to heal. Seek help, reach out, be bold. Never stop learning and growing on your journey to wellness and wholeness. (Cue: Beethoven's "Ode to Joy" music.)

"Music is life! No matter what we are going through, music makes everything better."

– CarolLynn Gregson

Susan Veenstra is an independent music teacher, small business owner, artist, and author. She is a classically trained pianist, the mother of three adult children, and an experienced educator. Susan has been inspired by countless "teachers" throughout her life, first her parents and then various members of her community. A former middle school language arts teacher, Susan's true passion is teaching music one-on-one and in small group settings. She believes that the visual arts are therapeutic and necessary for humans to thrive. She admires people who have overcome illness and obstacles through music and arts. Susan enjoys reading, writing, painting, quilting, and singing. She appreciates beauty in nature by gardening, hiking, and kayaking. Her interests include musical theater, American history, psychology, art therapy, and music therapy. Susan holds a master's degree in Special Education. She lives in St. Louis, Missouri with her husband, two dogs, and a cat.

susan.e.veenstra@gmail.com
www.veenstrakeyboardstudio.duetpartner.com

■

Meera Shekar, DNP, APRN, FNP-BC, NP-C

Mountains Survive Crisis but What Happens to Anthills?

A cough, a sniffle, a sore throat

Fever, chills, and malaise

A common cold? Or an unshakeable bronchitis?

A trip to the doctor

Negative for influenza and for strep

Then came the whiff of a news one did not want to hear

Is it, or isn't it?

Then the ruffled feathers, tremors, and the scent of fear

Pandemic—no way!!

This monstrous virus' escalating strength, not differentiating age, sex, class, or geographical boundaries, has crippled many resources, as well as mental and physical lives. How can one stand up against the strength of this virus which has infiltrated slowly across the borders of each country, ruthlessly damaging the countenance of each human being, destroying the core of stability, mental peace, and loving families? Not a whisper of precaution blowing to the ear yet consuming the fire of life from each and every human being. How could one prepare?

I practice alongside my husband who is a family physician. We quickly learned that adaptability is what made us and our practice stronger, more independent, and resilient. Innovative ways to overcome barriers became our strength and drive to survive.

I remember the confused feeling when I encountered a patient who had returned from abroad, who tested negative for all tests, flu, mono and strep. Yet that recurrent cough and incredible fatigue, just that little annoying sense of fear that crept in me, could it be the dreaded new virus?

We practice in St. Louis County, Missouri and we had not seen one case of the virus yet, nor were they testing. Here I was, working in a small private practice with my husband. Our days were consumed by seeing patients, an office with a busy staff and with medical students who were doing their family practice rotation with us. That fateful day, Friday, March 13th, 2020, I did not realize, would change the course of our secure routine. My husband came up to me midmorning and said, "I think I am shutting down the practice, we are in a pandemic!" That sinking feeling and my response "What, what do you mean? Are you sure, how are we going to take care of our patients?" He, with his calm demeanor, said, "Whether we accept it or not, I believe we have no option but to shut down. I am sure we will figure something out." We took the rest of the day off, asked our staff to stay home and we went home. Within the hour we figured the only way we could be of service and remain active in caring for our patients was to offer virtual visits. And thus, the course of life took a whole new turn.

We were able to keep our practice running. Income dwindled and our office workers had to claim unemployment benefits as the office was not operating at its full capacity. Uncertainty was escalating with increased cases and the worst: losing some of our patients who succumbed to the virus. Sharing that heartache with the families who lost so much, and more, was emotionally exhausting.

This increased my determination to be part of the vaccination program. I had applied really early for access to vaccines. Amidst many controversies, my husband and I both knew that it was the hope for a possible healthier future for all. Odd as it seemed, I got consumed in vaccinating with the sheer determination and expectation of keeping our community safe as much as possible, and at every available hour, while continuing to virtually see our patients. Many in the community silently showed up and got their vaccines. I personally made calls to many businesses in the neighborhood and was met with a list of those who were eligible to get the vaccines and then, there were some who were belligerent and scoffed at my offer, while questioning the need for the immunization. I even held mass events with the desire to vaccinate as many as I could.

Determined, I had joined the coalition of mass vaccination programs, and was very thankful for the government support we received in terms of getting our supplies to vaccinate in our community. In our small parking lot, I arranged for the cars to come in and wait while I vaccinated many individuals in their cars for the first round of vaccines. People were eager and the clinic started at six in the morning and sometimes ending at ten at night. There were days when we had seventy to eighty individuals who would come in a five-hour span. I devised a methodical system for checking them in and getting the vaccinations done smoothly. I was amazed at how some of them were afraid to let their family members know that they were getting vaccinated. When I offered a vaccine to a patient, one person angrily said, "do you even understand what EUA is, how are you giving it, what if someone loses the ability to have children or loses their mind?" to which I calmly answered, "yes I am aware that it is for *Emergency Use Authorization* and since many of us in this community are losing our near and dear ones, I feel it is appropriate. Since we are amidst a pandemic, do we not want to survive?" A couple of months later she informed me that she did get vaccinated. I had put up vaccine posters outside the building and they would magically disappear, but I repeated until the mischief maker tired.

Slowly, we were able to bring in our patients safely and surely with caution and offer hands-on care to the elderly. It might seem bewildering to many that we are still very cautious in offering appointments in person, yet one must realize our practice is one that is not under a corporate management agreement. Financially, we are not at our potential, yet it has been a blessing in many ways. Limiting the number of patients, and maintaining caution, has kept us afloat and alive.

Reflecting on the past two years, living in a world of caution, with uncertainty and apprehension, rising to the occasion of self-preservation seems to have kept our sanity. True to ourselves, following rules and regulations seem to have been the key to our survival, both physically and for our work environment.

Two things evolved to engulf us in comfort; primarily the kinship amidst our staff and secondly our patients, despite their vulnerable situations, who periodically checked on us while sharing their distress. We even had some of our patients provide us masks, sanitizers, and protective gear in the hope of keeping us safe. We have many patients from different parts of the world, it was noteworthy that cultural differences, if any, magically disappeared. There was this sense of one world, a feeling of one nation due to the insurmountable mental distress in which we were all placed. The stories that we shared, families losing loved ones, their jobs, and the distress from it all just somehow became more bearable.

As time was progressing towards the effects of the pandemic being somewhat in control, while conversing with patients, I sensed that the ego that was present in many of our patients, the sense of being "the one and only", somehow melted away. Our patients expressed their patience, if there was a sense of urgency, they were able to understand that the need of the others may have been more. Seldom did I hear a complaint; courtesy took over and there was an aura of peace despite melancholy and its rippled effects.

A small practice that we are, like an *anthill*, we too have learned to brave the storm. We may be miniscule compared to the corporate *mountain*-like managed health care system, and our story may not be that exciting. Learning to withstand the brutal force of this virus, getting things under control to harness the spread was, and will be, our goal. Truly thankful for the innate positive vibes and using our judicious caution, while warding away negativity, has let us do our own little part in this massive turmoil.

Resilience is the key to survival, and the strong motivation casting aside the surmounting negativity and carving a path of an innovative mode of operation, has kept us in our medical practice.

Dr. Meera Shekar is a family nurse practitioner. She is in a private practice in Kirkwood, Missouri. She has nearly 30 years of experience in the medical field. Her focus is on prevention, treatment of chronic and acute health issues for all ages. She believes the fundamentals to a healthy life start with mental and physical balance. In her earlier years she worked as a neonatal nurse and continues to have an affinity for maternal health and infants. Her love for teaching, being versatile, and her compassionate nature allows her to treat her patients to achieve their health goals.

She enjoys time with her husband, their four daughters, and their families. She loves to cook, garden, read, and craft at every opportunity. Her motto is, "Enjoy life as it comes, make every minute count!"

www.linkedin.com/in/dr-meera-shekar-ab70696
www.facebook.com/meera.shekar.1
www.twitter.com/meera4shekar
www.instagram.com/meera.shekar/

■

Donalee Gastreich

Listen, Learn, and Lead

One of my most valuable learnings in my life has been that of my PQ, my physical intelligence system. You have access to this intelligence too. PQ, is your ability to listen, identify and respond to internal messages about your physical self. Pain, hunger, depression, fatigue, and frustration are just some examples. In learning to listen, it has shown me that at my core is peace and happiness. It has taught me that everything is of some value, what is going on inside me and outside, what I think, feel, and say—and what I do not.

In January of 2020, I was invited to a seat in city council. Honored and ready, I said yes. I was ready for this new role in leadership, and I had a lot to learn about local government, various departments, the array of topics that came before council for approval, and the importance of voting on behalf of my constituents—to say things were busy was a gross under-statement. As with any new job, there were times of overwhelm, uncer-tainty, and frustration. I felt as if I was overly tapping into my coping skills like never before. Add to the busy-ness of this new part-time position, running my own business, my home, and life, I also needed to campaign for re-election in April, just a few months away.

The only campaigning I had done was asking local vendors for a donation for a school event or subdivision pool party. Campaigning for election was a whole new ballgame and I ... was in uncharted waters. I was deep in fear. Asking others for money to support my campaign was totally outside my comfort zone. I came from the belief that money was an exchange. And what was I giving? I had so many fears surfacing so fast, I could feel a part of me spiraling out of control. My go-to response was to do nothing. It is said fear causes us to freeze, flee, or fight; and Universal Law tells us that growth does not exist without conflict. Yet, I was frozen!

I can do this, I told myself over and over again. I had to remind myself of the inner strength and determination I had when doing other things in my life for the first time. I had to lean into the power within to Rise with Resilience. I had to pause and take notice of my focus, which was stuck on the fear. I had to STOP making fear my focus. I had to shift my focus to the outcome I wanted instead. I had to look at my options, my resources, my friends, businesses I serve in the community and those who already valued me. I reached out to other city council representatives for advice, referrals, and support. In knowing I can do this, I found the resilience and gained the support I needed, and raised nearly $4,000, enough to send out three mailings and put signage out in the community.

On March 7, 2020, at a Lincoln Day Banquet, I experienced an eerie early warning signal of something that was about to change the world. The keynote speaker cancelled; he was confirming the first case of the virus in St. Louis. Later the next day, this news was released, and by the end of that week, government authorities had declared all non-essential businesses to close, restaurants to shut their doors, offering pick-up or drive-thru only. Businesses put "work from home" orders in place. Schools closed. Everything shut down.

How we handle uncertainty and radical change is unique to each of us. It can range from fear, anxiety, and confusion to acceptance, adaptability, and agility. I cannot deny there was a part of me that was relieved; relieved of the busy-ness and chaos I had been caught in and relieved that I did not have to create the disruption to make it stop. You see, the hardest part in creating change is disrupting our old ways, habits, and patterns. My business, Complete Solutions, aids change and progress in businesses, and as with all advancement, disrupting the old ways and current structure is necessary to bring in the change. To unlearn and relearn what is necessary. I know how hard it is to disrupt and dismantle what exists in order to create something new—and part of me was okay in all of this.

But next, one by one my business clients canceled appointments and speaking and training contracts. My once loaded calendar was now empty. City council and networking groups quickly moved online. The companies I had been working with had decided to put their progress on hold to deal with the crisis before them. I went from an extremely busy life to no life in just one week. I went from feeling relieved by the shutdown to fearing how I would generate income.

I needed a plan. Two words popped into my head—Pivot and Adapt. I knew the way forward was not in fighting what was. Days, weeks, months passed with more of the same. Again, my response was to do nothing. I watched and things were not changing. I knew I had to go through the muck and messiness, to accept what is, and its effect on people, businesses, and communities. There was a deep depression in accepting what was happening. It felt so wrong to keep loved ones from their families, to allow anyone to die alone, and to close churches and places people go to for comfort. All I kept thinking was, *"What is this doing to those unskilled at monitoring, managing, and mastering their mind and emotions to bring themselves back into balance? What was this doing to those without coping skills?"*

With every trip outdoors, I was reminded of what was going on in the world. I could feel the fear as the masked world took extra care to make sure there was more than six feet between us. I felt the separation, the loneliness, and the disconnect. It was as though I could feel the suffering of others. I live alone and my circle of friends were not comfortable being around others. Never in my life have I felt so alone and withdrawn from the world. I felt the anxiety of empty shelves, even when I did not need what would have been on that shelf. I noticed myself reaching for comfort food. I had a lack of discipline in my decision making. I was suffering just like everyone else. I guess I thought I was immune to all the effects of what was happening.

Aware that I needed to focus on my own health and well-being, on what I can do to keep myself strong and healthy, I could not stop thinking about others in my community. I was so confused as to why no one was talking about how to build a strong immune system, prevent or manage the stress of what our current environment created, and simple steps to well-being. All the messages from CDC, WHO, and our government were messages of mandates, fear, masking, and social distancing from others. Surely, I thought a Center for Disease Control looks at what it takes to have good health. Of course, the World Health Organization will tell the people ways to be of sound mental and emotional health during these challenging times or ways to reduce stress and anxiety. No one was saying anything.

My position in city council gave me a bigger picture view on the well-being of the community. The homeless numbers climbed. The children, both in school and virtual, were showing signs of stress, anxiety, and depression. Health care workers and teachers had unbelievable stress in their workday, and it was environmental stress - stress from outside them. Everyone was affected. No one was exempt from the damaging and disruptive effects that the fear, worry and social distancing created in the psyche, memory, and nervous system of every human being. We were all under the spell of this deep conditioning.

It was not until the summer of 2020, after the election, when I was forced to focus on me. I had put all my energy, all my focus on the city council position, so much so, that I neglected my business and my personal well-being. I did not win the election. I woke up the day after, with a deep emptiness and an "okay, now what" attitude. Life does not always deliver exactly what we expect, but I knew it was delivering what I needed. Even if I could not see it yet. I had been through enough of life disappointments to know that they almost always end up working out better than I could have imagined. In the weeks that followed, I reflected on all that the position had awarded me, shown me, and how it had grown me.

I was changed. You have been changed. I had quit walking every day. I was sitting before a computer for hours. My old practices of meditation, yoga, being in nature, connecting with friends and family, socializing, parties, and BBQs were no longer a part of my life. It was as if the computer was my last thread of connection to others and I was glued to it. This is not my choice or desire. Things had to change. I had to start building back a new way of life that was nurturing and fulfilling my needs and connection with others.

Within every human being is a powerful energy we call RESILIENCE, it is the capacity to recover quickly from difficulties, it is a toughness, a determination of sorts. In time, my own inner strength brought me back to where I wanted to be and more. I got clarity on all I had learned, my purpose, and my next steps. Through this experience, I birthed a book, *Bringing Spirituality into Business: Your Guide to Know Yourself, Grow Yourself, to Live Life Empowered*. It is scheduled to be released Summer, 2022.

In the year that followed the pandemic, I created and let go of so many things. When you believe in yourself you can make anything happen. My greatest lesson was learning to *Listen* to my PQ, to *Learn* from that listening, and to *Lead* myself with confidence and clarity to more. With every ending is the start and beginning of something new. You have a power inside you that is greater than you know. You have the powerful potential to *Rise with Resilience*. Your spiritual intelligence is always showing you there is more for you, that you are more than this situation, and that you can triumph, succeed, and excel. It is my hope that you allow yourself to recover from life's difficulties and Listen, Learn, and Lead yourself to more.

Donalee Gastreich is a Speaker, Trainer, Difference Maker, and founder at Complete Solutions. She is a lover of life and a life-time learner. She is also spontaneous, an explorer by nature and she loves variety.

Her passion for health, fitness, and well-being began back in the 1980's with her lifetime membership to Vic Tanny. She's always been focused on being the best version of HERSELF. With books like "The Power of Positive Thinking" and self-help gurus as mentors, she would delve into cassettes while driving. Donalee admits she may have been labeled a type-A personality back then.

Her life has been a roller coaster ride of ups and downs, experiencing some dark times and much joy and celebration. She came to realize in those challenging times both her struggle to hold on to the pain and her struggle to let it go. And it was through this, Donalee learned to Listen, Learn and Lead herself to something more. She believes the three greatest gifts we can give ourselves is to know ourselves, grow ourselves, and live our lives empowered.

Donalee believes there is Greatness in every human life and that we are all on a journey to uncover and recognize this within ourselves.

www.Donalee360.com

■

Amy Holder, MSN, APRN, FNP-BC

Silence

I recall the Latino girl in the 1985 movie, *A Chorus Line*. She stepped out in front of the line of the others when it was her turn to sing. With strength, but reserve, she sang loudly. Her song was about a young girl in a music class trying to work with imagery. The professor would show an image, and the students would have to imagine and dig deep to feel all the sensations in the story. The purpose of this improv imagery exercise was for students to properly experience the mood and the feeling to "get" the experience without truly experiencing it fully in real life.

I watched that movie so many times. My sister and I knew all the songs and dances by heart. But the Latino girl's song particularly always stuck with me. She wanted to be like the others in the class who got it, felt it, and she really did try. In frustration she cried out, "So, I dug right down to the bottom of my soul to see what I had inside. Yes, I dug right down to the bottom of my soul. Yes, I tried! Nothing! I felt nothing! Except that this bullshit was absurd." She could never feel the *"whoosh"* and see any of this imagery—all she saw was nothingness.

I _never_ felt the calmness inside or heard the silence in my head as others say they can feel or hear. As a younger girl and through most of my adult life, I have lived a hard, chaotic, and hectic life, from finding a pair of matching socks to finding good relationships. My brain was a constant battlefield between good guys and bad guys. I always had to stay busy because the silence hurt my ears. I always felt like something was missing in my life and I yearned for that peacefulness that others often say they have inside.

However, all this changed in August 2020. This is the summer when I finally got to feel peace, stillness, calm, and quiet. For the past 20 years, I had three kids, a marriage, and a Family Nurse Practitioner career. We all know there was no silence during this time. I found myself once again submerged in my job. Crazy days and crazy nights in one of the busiest emergency rooms in St. Louis, MO. In my heart I felt like I was doing good work taking care of the sick people in the emergency room, but I could not find that work/home life balance. I felt horrible leaving home to take care of others that I did not know when my family was remotely ill. And let us be honest, did those sick people I was taking care of in the emergency room (who did not know me), did they even appreciate me?

Then the virus came. I was so afraid to go to work and be exposed, and then possibly exposing my family. In the beginning of the pandemic, we were unsure of EVERYTHING! The infectious virus doctors speculated on four things: having us work in an enclosed trailer for 12-hours and seeing patients exposed to the virus, while wearing the proper equipment and using air purifiers, that our risk of being contaminated was low. *They speculated!*

Please trust me on this: it is super scary when you count on equipment and others to provide the correct information that may save your life and that of your family. For months I was donning and doffing and showering after working 12-hour shifts—all the while not knowing if this was going to protect me and my family.

On top of this stress, I was worried about my ill patients. With most of them virus-positive, were they going to live or die? *Healthcare workers care immensely about their patients!* Leaving our families at home to work our shifts, we are taking care of and serving, complete strangers. I am willing to do this for my patients, risk my life for them every shift. Call it crazy, stupid, or genuine. It is who I am - true, honest, and dedicated.

One day, after a long eight-hour shift, I received a call on my work phone from my manager's secretary. I was asked if I could do a Zoom call with both managers and one emergency room finance executive. I thought this was odd, but reluctantly agreed. We Zoom conferenced while I was on the parking lot, in my car, before driving home for the day. I was told, because of the low census in the Emergency Room, and the fact that the Emergency Department was losing money, they were forced to furlough a group of Emergency Room providers. *I was chosen to be FURLOUGHED!*

On the upside, being furloughed meant a break from the virus exposure. On the downside, it meant no more patients ... and no job. I loved my patients and I loved what I was doing for our community.

Of course, all the questions came ... *why me?* What did I do or not do? But those were not the right questions at the time. That was May 28, 2020. For the next two months, I cried and was depressed. I felt lonely. While everyone seemed to be moving along, I was paralyzed in the same position.

Up to this point in life, I have always been the girl that would break dance in the living room for no reason, or bust out the McHammer just because I felt happy that day? Now I was low. I lost myself, my purpose, my career. I could not believe I missed taking care of the public so much when half the time they yelled at me or did not appreciate me! Valid feelings for sure.

A month later, I decided to stop being a chronic martyr. I needed to pull myself together for my family. I began by trying to settle the chaos in my brain doing yoga at home to feel calmer and more peaceful. I was enjoying yoga so much that I advanced to warm and hot yoga at studios around St. Louis. I loved the peaceful feeling of the Savasana pose at the end of the class. It was at this point that I realized yoga helps me be resilient. When I realized I could actually feel peace, I decided to try meditation.

Meditation is where I finally found my silence and inner peace! I bought an app on my phone and started with beginner guided meditation.

It worked out wonderfully! I learned about basic meditation techniques, postures and my app even had cognitive behavior therapy and life coaching! Meditation helped advance my yoga experience too.

I started to gain control of my life again and I felt great. I could use meditation anywhere and in any situation. I started hiking all the time and meditating while hiking. I got an app on my phone that showed my nearby hiking spots in my zip code, and I mapped out places I wanted to visit. I went on day trips to these places alone or with family. It was so refreshing! *I began Rising with Resilience.*

Many people say the pandemic has taken so much from us. Which it has. At the same time, the pandemic has also given me something back, something I chased for years. That something is my sanity and some inner peace.

I may not have watched *A Chorus Line* during the pandemic, yet that song has always been within me. It took a virus, a pandemic and being furloughed to help me find and sing my own song.

Amy Holder, MSN, APRN, FNP-BC has spent 22 years in critical care within hospitals and outpatient settings. She believes in blending medical practices to achieve optimal health. Amy's greatest joy in her work is taking care of people.

Amy is married with three children. She spends much of her free time with her family. She enjoys traveling, hiking, yoga, and meditation.

It took a virus, a pandemic and being furloughed to help her find and sing her own song. Her wish for everyone is that they, too, find their own personal song.

www.facebook.com/amy.gusmanholder

■

Jenny Grace Morris

Shining Through The Mist

Passover and Easter celebrations were joyously placed on my calendar. I love the significance of these Holidays. It is a treasure being with people, eating foods specifically prepared for the occasion, and hearing spiritual stories. I had four siblings and there was very little time spent alone. That changed when we went our separate ways with everyone getting married, at least once, with the exception of me. As an adult living far away from family, and in a city where people seemed to know one another before they were even born, my new family developed through organizational acquaintances.

Sadly, I received an email that the 2020 Passover Seder was canceled due to a global pandemic. Inspired by the Passover story, I placed a printed copy of the 91st Psalm on my front door.

Years earlier, my daughter left home, leaving her bedroom empty. I knew that living alone was not for me. If anything breaks down, or there is a new item in the house that requires technology or mechanical skill, it will remain broken or in the box till someone with the slightest ability in those areas comes to visit. I was praying for a solution to missing my daughter when the opportunity to host a foreign exchange student came by email. I happen to enjoy the company of highschoolers, except for rebellious teens. Providentially, I was not asked to host someone from my own country.

The State department's YES program was the perfect answer to my prayers. I was the host mom to a brilliant young girl from Bangladesh. I loved having her so much that a year later (2019-2020) I hosted a student from Albania.

We were looking for prom dresses when the virus forced her school to close, and the prom was canceled.

We were equally anxious, waiting impatiently for the plans for her early departure. I projected the dreaded loneliness I would encounter once she left. The sad day came in April 2020 and almost immediately my daughter moved back into her bedroom. This did nothing to help my loneliness since she was the epitome of a deep thinker who preferred solitude, and our daily interaction was sparse. I was fortunate to see her a few minutes every three days. It made me envious of introverts who could function easily without any desire to socialize.

I always start my day in prayer and refrain from outlining how God will provide a solution to my prayers, but let the inspirational solution come to me. During these endless weeks of isolation, my mother called every morning so I would feel loved. Then she told me to pray for a single, rich, and handsome man to knock on my door. Humored by the thought, I still had to rise with resilience and lavished myself with inhouse activities. I spent much time listening to podcasts or reading articles on Christianity and its healing effect on contagion. There is no purpose in doing anything if it cannot be applied to real life, which was evident when my dear friend's daughter was quarantined in their house for a few weeks. Unfortunately, that meant her household was under quarantine. While praying for the family, the word "food" came to mind, so a mutual friend and I, fully covered with highly protective gear (that in previous years would have made us look like criminals) went food shopping. We drove to our friend's home, placed the bags of healthy items on her porch, rang the doorbell, ran back to the car, and waved our hands as she saw the packages. She smiled wide once she recognized the mysterious bell ringers.

A colleague mentioned that her son needed a place to stay for a few weeks in the summer. During one of my mornings *"listening to God's plan for me"* moments, I heard distinctly that I was to offer her son my condominium for several weeks. I replied in prayer, *"Ok, but where am I supposed to go?"* Immediately the response was, you and your daughter will visit the National Parks. It was something I had contemplated over the years, but since I dislike long distance driving, and the idea of encountering unusual species in the wild, I had not taken it seriously. Yet, out of my mouth came the question to my daughter, "How about going on a National Parks tour?" More surprising was her response. "Sure." Indubitably this was God's plan. It seems that even an extreme introvert needs a little sunshine.

Hiking through the parks was a triumph! My mind and feet do not always communicate, but I tenaciously climbed up and down the mountains and rejoiced that I remained intact. The confidence received by moving beyond my comfort zone served me well. The rental of a log cabin in the woods is a perfect example of overcoming my fear of being in a dark secluded place.

Driving home, I pondered on the upcoming prolonged social distancing. My cute and playful dog, Snowball, was good company, but did not quench my need for conversation. My daughter, like a bear preparing for winter, was ready to hibernate. While medical professionals were working diligently around the clock, people like me longed for more activity and dialogue. Thankfully, my social circle started online book clubs. Our church provided gatherings, via zoom, by reading the Bible sermon or articles from the media prompting us to pray for the world. I continued to send out Biblical promises of healing to those requesting prayers and asking God what more I could do.

The Gateway to Dreams director created an annual workshop called *Joy Of Goals* and asked me if I would co-create a Christ-centered version that would bless Christian corporations and churches. I eagerly accepted this assignment, letting endeavors like this take the place of socialization.

During the pandemic, several life coaches interviewed me on zoom about my business' *Clarify Your Calling: Embrace the Role You were Born to Play*. Also, a radio host interviewed me regarding my part in re-enacting Susan B. Anthony for *Voices Of American Herstory*. I also wrote a chapter for an Anthology titled *Living Your tRuth (in honor of Ruth Bader Ginsburg)*. Coming up with a topic was challenging, and I prayed till an idea was illuminated. If I had not been sheltering in place, would those interviews have been available to me?

Several sick and fearful people asked me to pray for them. I sent them Biblical verses on healing. When I started having chills and fever, I prayed, but kept feeling worse. Considering that we were experiencing a global pandemic, could it be possible that God's mailbox was full? Of Course not, Divine Love is infinite. I contemplated if I truly believed the Psalmist's prose, "No plague can come nigh thy dwelling" or the words from Jeremiah, "For I will restore Health unto thee."

My faith gets challenged in difficult circumstances. I start to doubt the efficacy of my prayers. I am tempted to forget my faith and resign to feelings of hopelessness. In this scenario, I wanted to prevail. I thought of the Proverb "*Wisdom is the principal thing; with all thy getting, get understanding.*" I contacted a church member to pray for me. She emphatically stated that I was not alone. God/Love was right there with me. Complete recovery came quickly, and my faith was restored.

My daughter developed a highly contagious disease and was in immense pain. I suggested she go to the hospital the following morning, but she could also ask for dedicated prayer from a Christian healer. All she wanted was relief, not religion, and said, "Sure, but can you call her because I don't have the energy?" The woman I contacted requested that I have full confidence in the power and presence of God who as a *"Mother comforteth Her children"* (Isaiah 66). Much to my daughter's astonishment, all her symptoms disappeared by morning. We both had risen with resilience by placing our trust in a higher power.

Determined to utilize alone time effectively, I listened for each step, one building on the other. Our *Women of American Herstory* was filmed. I became a recurrent registrant, enrolling in the *National Speakers Academy*, numerous Bible studies, and a voice acting course. This last venture was my passion. When reading aloud, participants would urge me to become a voice over artist. Thinking back to sharing my desire to be a voice actor in earlier years, the response was often, *"Who would hire you?"* This unfulfilled dream was to be a reality. Now, I replaced those words with the affirmation *"I am talented, God gave me a gift to use for a good purpose."* I claimed my victory when businesses offered me jobs.

The list of challenges to be overcome, and the abundance of successful activities removed lonely moments. Ideally, it would bring me solace to actively seek solutions to life's bewildering moments and celebrate achievements with another person, but for now my dog, Snowball, and Zoom, and new opportunities were the answer to my prayers. It is amazing what you can accomplish when the only exciting part of your week is a trip to the grocery store. Now I saw greater visions on the horizon, and honestly, found myself Rising with Resilience.

Jenny Grace Morris is an author, voice actor, Clarity Coach and Mom. She began writing when asked to create speeches, presentations and workshops for conferences and international summits. She also emcee's for events and co-hosts the monthly meeting *Write your book Right now for Gateway to Dreams.* She created a BLOG called *Ask Amazing Grace* for an online news source called *Wilmington Faith and Values,* which answered questions on faith and daily living. Although this news bureau no longer exists, the questions keep coming in, and so the BLOG continues.

Jenny Grace just completed filming her Re-enactment of Susan B. Anthony for Voices of American Herstory.

Her favorite activity is creating voices for characters in books, scripts, and copy.

askamazinggrace@gmail.com
jennygracemorris.com
jennygracevoiceacting@gmail.com
www.USAherstory.com
www.facebook.com/jennygraceinspire
www.linkedin.com/in/jennygracemorris

■

Carrie Burggraf

A Matter of Life and Death

Having a child is often seen as a highlight in a human life. Childbirth itself is messy and painful, but also full of immense meaning and love. There is a feeling of fear going into the childbirth experience, the unknown, and a huge release at the end. Childbirth lifts the veil on the connection between us and the Universe, God and being. It helps us identify what is *real* and makes us realize how many other things in our lives simply aren't important in comparison. Childbirth creates an incredible mirror for our lives.

Ironically, death is the same—a pivotal moment in a human life. It is messy and painful, full of immense meaning and, in time, on the other side of the suffering, is love. There is a feeling of fear going into the dying experience and a huge release at the end. It lifts the veil on the connection between us and the Universe, God and being. Death helps us realize how many seemingly important things in our lives don't really matter and creates an incredible mirror for our lives.

The pandemic has given us a new appreciation for the privileges we've taken for granted and an experience of threat to life and of death in a way that most of us have never experienced—the almost invisible but constant and widespread risk; the surprising vulnerability of young and old, healthy and not; the sheer volume of the sick, dying, and dead; the isolation, unknown to us in this way prior to 2020. Watching teammates get up every day and jump back into this altered world has been nothing short of inspiring. There is a cumulative exhaustion for all, but particularly among the caregiving ranks of those responding to the virus as teams navigate the demands, the protocols, the staffing limitations, the lack of available resources, the fear, and the losses.

As a geriatric physician's assistant whose mother founded the hospice in my hometown, loss in the form of death is not new to me. But what a privilege to be invited into those moments with families and patients, to have the opportunity to hopefully ease the transition and support those present. One family I worked with was having the incredibly difficult experience of a 45-year-old daughter whose breast cancer had spread to her brain, bones, and liver. She was on hospice in the skilled nursing facility where I was working. Every Friday I would leave work, certain that she would not be alive when I returned Monday. And for many months, she was. Her mother often suggested that perhaps the cancer was gone, it had been a long time since the diagnosis, maybe something had changed, should we run more tests to see? She, of course, wanted so much for this not to be happening for her daughter.

One cold winter evening as I was leaving the facility, the mother stopped me in the doorway, the room dark and dimly lit by a lamp in the corner. She said she wanted to ask me a question. She said with such vehemence, "I hate God so much right now!" And then more quietly, "Do you think he'll ever forgive me?" I felt the sounds in the facility drop away, the air become electrified, the hairs on my arms stand. I assured her that God understood completely, and that He was present and loving her and her daughter this very moment. She cried softly and a few days later, her daughter finally passed. The care her daughter received was important but the support that families need in those kinds of moments is what gives jobs in the healthcare field meaning.

About ten years ago, my father had bypass surgery, replacing several vessels in his heart during a long and tenuous surgery. In the two weeks following, his heart went into a potentially fatal rhythm *twenty times*! It was incredibly stressful to ride the waves of hearing "Code Blue" in his

ICU room while we sat in the waiting room, knowing they were shocking his heart to attempt to reverse the dangerous rhythm. We would conclude that he was passing and prepare ourselves for that reality when they would come to tell us that he survived.

Months later, when he was home improving and reflecting on the experience with me, he apologized for the stress that those weeks must have put on all of us. As I thought of how to respond to him, I realized something. I understood for the first time that while I have always loved my father, I have never loved him *more* than during and since those weeks. Clearly, he was the one who suffered those huge medical challenges, so he bore the brunt of the pain. But how could I regret a time that allowed me to value someone at an even greater level than I had in the past?

Recently I called home to see how my parents were doing. Dad informed me that Mom had been struggling with food poisoning for the last three weeks. People don't really have food poisoning for three weeks, so I told Dad that Mom needed to go to the hospital. She was resistant, he said, because they were afraid of being exposed to and contracting the virus, but the next day she finally agreed to go. (Many people are trying to manage significant and threatening illness at home to avoid the virus, often at the risk of dying from other diseases). She was diagnosed with acute myelogenous leukemia and transferred to a larger hospital. I headed to them the next day.

On the way, her oncologist called to confirm the diagnosis and said that, without treatment, she had two weeks left to live. Mom, 92, had always said she would never do chemotherapy and given her current symptoms, I doubted she would even tolerate treatment. Due to her significant hearing loss, she was unaware of her diagnosis and prognosis, and my dad didn't have the heart to tell her. I said I would tell her when I got there in a few hours.

After visiting for a couple of hours, my brother took Dad to dinner and home. I sat with Mom, rubbing cream into her hands and legs, a favorite activity for her. I then got a legal pad from my bag and wrote out the details of her situation and handed it to her. She read through the pages carefully, stopping only to look up at me with some surprise to say, "Two weeks?" I nodded and said, "I know." One of the hardest moments of that whole time was matching her reaction and not crying, because I didn't want her to feel the need to take care of me.

She read the pages through once more and sat quietly for a moment. I had written at the end of the pages, "What questions do you have? What can I do for you?" Then she asked me if I could do several things. First, could the family help her decide whether to attempt chemotherapy? Of course— we would support whatever she chose to do. Second, we would need to contact the hospice company she founded, because they would be needed, "sooner or later". Finally, she said, we needed to hire a housekeeper, because Dad will never be able to keep up with the house alone. She also asked if she could go on hospice and go home the next day. Absolutely.

"Oh, you can do one more thing for me? Could you go get us each a glass of wine?" With the nurse's permission, I went across the street and got a bottle of wine. When I got back and was pouring the wine into Styrofoam cups, I asked how she was doing. She said with a smile that she was making a list of *all* the things she no longer needed to do. We sat and drank the wine and talked about her feelings until she fell asleep. I was not allowed to spend the night, so I returned to my parents' home and came back the next day. That morning she was in a much different state and said, "Am I really going to do this for two weeks?" She struggled somewhat through that day and night, not with pain but restlessness. The oncologist had provided orders that allowed us to ask for whatever we needed to make her comfortable.

The next day, Mom passed with my brother and me at her side, always a model of insane efficiency. My brother and I, twins, were also born on Mom's birthday. The three of us were together at the beginning of my life and the three of us were together at the end of hers. We talked to her about what an amazing mother she had been, how we would have her with us forever, and that we would take great care of each other, especially Dad.

Her death, like her life, like all our lives, was messy and difficult, but overflowing with meaning and so much love.

Apple Pie Dying

How I wish I had been with her
As she measured the flour and the salt,
Cut in the shortening
And sprinkled on water,
Balling the dough,
Rolling it out, lifting it--
Peeling the apples, slicing them,
Spicing them and crimping the crust,
Listening to Paul Harvey or Cokie Roberts
Or Oprah in the background,
Mopping the floor and changing the beds,
Filling the birdfeeder while the pastries were baking,
Then cooling, being basketed and backseated
And on to the church.

Oh, with her as she delivered them,
Two pies to the women saying, "Bless you!"

With her as she closed that door and opened another,
Falling past the pavement and onto green grass
Which cushioned her clean slacks and blue shirt,

Her last breath trembling a lavender impatiens

Which her own pie fingers had planted just one week before.

Oh, to have been there,
to have been there,
to have been there,

To have learned how to die.

Barbara Smith/Mom

Carrie Burggraf is a geriatric physician's assistant, certified geriatric care manager, technical writer, and business consultant for Wide Awake Business.

Carrie is passionate about whatever brings each person's greatest self to the world. This shows up in her work as a business consultant, specializing in sales analysis, as well as training and mentoring in the field for professional sales teams and selling service teams. Carrie and her diverse team of business consultants at Wide Awake Business empower small to medium-sized business owners and leaders so they build easier, simpler, and more profitable businesses.

Carrie is the mother of three grown sons and loves anything interactive and creative: fashion, design, cooking, writing, and speaking events.

Carrie@wideawakebusiness.com
www.linkedin.com/in/carrieburggraf/
www.facebook.com/carrie.burggraf.9

■

Maria Rodgers O'Rourke

A New Morning

There's a story about a farmer who was walking through his field one day, when he came across a bird lying on his back with his legs straight up in the air. Checking to see if the bird was alive, he asked, "Are you okay? Can't you fly?"

The bird replied, "I heard that the sky is falling and I'm trying to stop it."

"What makes you think," the farmer said, laughing, "that your skinny little legs will hold up the sky?"

The bird thought for a moment and said, "Well, I must do what I can."

In my *Rising with Resilience* story, I'm like that bird, doing what I can. And his winged friends are helping me find my way. Through the pandemic's upheaval and change, I discovered a sanctuary in my own backyard.

Considering the crises on the world stage, this shift might not seem like much. The world is in chaos. Our culture seems to value conflict over cooperation, winning over compassion, and separation over community. We're working harder than ever, sometimes wearing our busyness like a badge of honor. Millions of us are grieving losses of loved ones, jobs, homes, etc. In this heartbreaking overwhelm of the daily news, how can one woman make a difference?

When the stay-at-home order came down, my day-to-day life didn't change much in my home office. In fact, my work increased, thankfully, working for a client funding on-the-ground services for people in crisis, and training for an editor's certification. Yet, as the weeks dragged on, the fear and upheaval of the world's new normal got to me. I woke in the mornings dreading the day ahead, then doom-scrolled on my phone till it was time to get up. Some days, that took a while.

To stay informed, I compulsively read the news. I thought this was the right thing to do. I was worried for my family, friends, and myself. As the weeks went by, I came to see how the divisive and frightening news drained me. Rather than empowering me, I felt more tired after looking at my phone than I did when I first woke up. The phone poured pain and despair over me, and I let it.

With nowhere to go, I rediscovered our small yard and deck. On nice days, I worked outside on my laptop. On video calls, my colleagues commented on the sweet songs in the background. I too heard the birds, as if for the first time. Their songs lifted my tired heart. I wanted more of that feeling, instead of despair, so I began to start my days earlier. As the sun rose, you'd find me on the deck with my mug of tea, listening to the birds sing.

After a day or two, I wondered who was doing the singing? I could identify robins and cardinals by sight, sparrows, too. But, by song? Here's where my phone shifted from bad news source to partner in joy. I downloaded the BirdNet app, which knows the birds who inhabit my region of the world. I record a snippet of song, and BirdNet does the rest. Now I know without looking when a wren, or a Carolina Chickadee, or a Mourning Dove is nearby.

My *Rising with Resilience* story goes beyond the basics of birding, though. These daily meditations with the wee musicians have led me, in the words of poet David Whyte, to "see with every turning day, how each season makes a child of you again, wants you to become a seeker after rainfall and birdsong." I look forward to my early mornings now.

The evenings, too, have become occasions for bird encounters. Cooking yet another dinner at home last summer, a cardinal nestled in a tree beside the deck, chirping ever more slowly as the sun set. He returned every evening to sing himself to sleep. I'd tiptoed to the back door, and listened softly, barely breathing, for that sweet joy to touch my heart.

J. Drew Lanham, an ornithologist, professional birder, and poet, shares his experience this way:

> *In that moment of that little brown bird that's always so inquisitive, that sings reliably, in that moment that I'm think-ing about that wren, I'm not thinking about anything else. That's joy. And so sometimes, I think, we have to recognize the joy that the world didn't give us and that the world can't take away, in the midst of the world taking away what it can.*

One July morning, the birds' song broke through to poetry of my own. I sat on the deck, sipping my tea, anxiously thinking about the day ahead. A cool, damp breeze touched my skin. A wren perched in a tree close by, repeating a sweet riff:

> *I am here.*
> *I sing of the sun.*
> *Easing into the day*
> *Sure of more music to come.*

His gentle refrain distracted my cluttered mind. Then, a cacophony of blue jays swarmed in, their argument upstaging the wren. My critical mind cried with the blue jays:

> *This is hard.*
> *Clear the path.*
> *The To-Do's on my list are the problem. Oh, to be rid of these.*

The blue jays took off in a flurry, and the wren's sweet song lifted on the breeze, again.

Too often I abandon my heart's wren song to the blue jay caws. This day, the wren prevailed, and offered a new path for my thoughts to take. My inner poet responded:

Take my hand and we'll
dance with the wren atop the
picket fence
of the day's tasks
and together we shall sing
we shall sing
we shall sing

We've lived in our home for nearly 30 years, which sits on a modest quarter-acre corner lot in suburban Saint Louis County. We've spent many warm spring evenings there—or fall nights around the fire pit. During the pandemic, the birds invited me to *Rise with Resilience* and greet the dawn, too. This once-dreaded time of day has become my go-to spot for creativity and joy. The birds' songs have consoled and quieted my heart during a time when just surviving from day-to-day felt like a great accomplishment.

Nick Wignall writes that resilience has three components: Acceptance, Purpose, and Flexibility. The little bird in the farmer's field demonstrates all of these. He's accepted that big changes are coming, he's identified a way he can help, and he's willing to change his usual modus operandi in response. In my pilgrimage to my own backyard, I've discovered my own form of resilience. Like that little bird, I'm aware of the crisis, but now I'm out there doing what I can to help, instead of letting the news trap me in hopelessness. Plus, I finished that editor certification, sitting on my deck, with a song in my heart and on the breeze. I still catch myself scrolling on my phone for too long, sometimes. A quick moment outside sets me right again.

My *Rising with Resilience* story is important, even though it seems small, and was played out in a relatively comfortable setting. I wish I could walk out on the world stage and stop the pain and suffering. In my small way, holding space for joy and creativity, I'm contributing to that healing. We must all be intentional in noticing and affirming what's beautiful in our world. This practice lifts us all up. Songbirds sing "like they know the score" —Fleetwood Mac has been telling me this for years. Now, finally, I'm listening.

Maria Rodgers O'Rourke is a writer, speaker, and editor who also serves in nonprofit communications. A certified Story Grid Editor, Maria is a gifted wordsmith and developmental editor who delights in helping individuals and organizations tell their stories. Her professional experience began in advertising and public relations, moved to nonprofit leadership, and homed in on communications and writing when she completed her master's degree in pastoral studies.

Maria is publisher and author of two women's journals. She's a contributing columnist to the *St. Louis Post Dispatch, Suburban Journals, St. Louis Globe-Democrat*, the HuffPost, and has been published in the popular *Chicken Soup for the Soul* collections.

Maria's known for her warmth, wisdom, and humor which shine through in her workshops, retreats, and coaching. Maria and her husband Steve have two adult daughters and enjoy music, traveling, hiking, wineries, Wordle, and Cardinals baseball.

Visit MariaRodgersORourke.com for Maria's writings and events
Visit MROCommunications.com for Maria's editing and coaching services

www.facebook.com/MRodgersORourke
www.linkedin.com/in/mariarodgersorourke/
www.twitter.com/MariaMuse
www.instagram.com/mariarodgersorourke/

Carla Beckerle, DNP, APRN-BC

A Journey in Gratitude

As an incredibly young child, I knew I was going to become a nurse when I grew up. My aunt was very influential in my life and was a nurse in the Navy Corps. I was told I dressed as a nurse, at age three, on Halloween night as a tribute to her. She was my mentor and hero for many years and for that I am grateful since she helped to shape my future.

As I followed my true nature, I realized I had a propensity for the sciences and excelled in most. Even today, I have always had a quest for learning. Currently I teach doctoral students in a nursing program which extends this quest. I am grateful my avocation and vocation are realized daily.

As the oldest of five children, I knew education was also important to my parents. My father worked three jobs to save for our future education. I remember him saying he expected his "girls" to get an education so they could take care of themselves. I translated his expectations into his confidence in his "girls" for success in life by using our intellect to be independent adults. For his message, I am grateful. All five siblings have college degrees or post graduate degrees resulting from our father's expectations.

I also knew I could not go away to college and "play." So, I did not. I started nursing school, married, and had a daughter in short order, while working part time as a nurse in the intensive care unit of a local hospital. I soon knew I wanted to complete my bachelors and master's degrees. So very wisely, we had another child, a son, sleeping four hours a night and trying to "do it all." Those years were a whirlwind and gave me an opportunity to hone the skills of multi-tasking and goal setting. Thus, beginning my path of *Rising with Resilience!*

I loved the practice of critical care and emergency care and was a natural leader. I was able to garner leadership skills from mentors in nursing who were in leadership roles and who also loved the nursing profession. I regularly precepted students and nurses new to the profession, and supported their dreams, acknowledged their fears, and protected them from negativity in the workplace.

I worked in a variety of leadership roles and enjoyed creating innovative programs that enhanced patient care. After deciding to apply for the first nurse practitioner (NP) program in Saint Louis, MO, I began a journey of discovery that opened my eyes and filled my soul with joy! I could impact people in a wholistic and loving way as a nurse practitioner. I continued to love my vocation and used my leadership skills to influence policy and evidence-based care at the bedside for many years. I am grateful for my intellect and use it to make decisions that serve others.

Once again leaning into my true nature, I began a doctoral program a few years later. This education helped me understand the world of medicine and the implications for practice, the responsibility to mentor continuously, and the satisfaction of shaping policy and programs, and caring for patients with continuing passion. My experiences in the medical mission field across the globe afforded me additional appreciation for healthcare needs for those with no resources or infrastructure for healthcare. I am grateful for those who mentored me in this process and friends who understood my musings during those challenging times.

During the years that followed my doctorate, I moved into a strategic leadership position in my healthcare organization that currently has 45 offices and greater than 200 providers. My focus during the early years of my role was on the development of a multidisciplinary medical support team that offered wrap around services for the providers, patients, and office teams. These professionals created a safety net for the vulnerable and frail patients we served. This work required many hours of relentless focus during all hours of the day and night. I am grateful for my husband and children who always encourage me to be me and follow my true nature.

Then came an ugly virus, early in 2020, that changed the way everyone looked at the world around them. The past two years have been long and arduous. It is difficult to describe the many losses and suffering. As a health care provider, I have experienced a plethora of emotions related to this Pandemic that began in 2019 and continues into 2022.

My first response to the virus as it began in 2019, was planning for safety for myself, my family, and my patients, by developing a plan with the leadership team of our healthcare organization to test for the virus, then vaccinate providers, employees, and patients. This plan included offering testing and vaccinations to family and friends of patients also. It required many hours of coordination and volunteer hours from all segments of our healthcare organization. Safety products, like gloves and masks, were procured quickly so the teams providing testing and vaccinations could function in a safe manner. The shortage of cleaning supplies and personal hygiene products was surprising and a challenge to all segments of the United States. A variety of changes were made to provide care virtually as well as face-to-face care for our patients. These new processes took an emotional toll on all.

I lost my brother-in law, my nephew, and my father during the second year of the pandemic. There was no straightforward way to honor their lives since funerals and wakes had changed to quarantine and social distancing – all due to this ugly virus. Grieving was blunted. Isolation was the norm. Many lives were lost due to the virus, and multitudes of healthcare workers suffered from these losses emotionally and physically. A generation of health care professionals has nearly been destroyed by their experiences with this pandemic. Yet I am still grateful! My father was able to die in his own home during the pandemic, with his wife and other family members at his side. His death was from cancer and not from the virus, and it hurts no less. I am grateful for my parents who demonstrated lives of honor, integrity, and optimism and gave me the guidance and support to be the same.

During 2022 my ability to be resilient allowed me to focus and find ways to support wellness for the employees and patients of our healthcare organization. Our mental health support programming flourished and was offered weekly to those who chose to participate. Observing the behavioral health team responses for patients needing a lifeline, this support program makes me grateful that I am trusted to make decisions that impact patients and families in a meaningful way.

The year of 2022 brings my nuclear family a new set of challenges. Our mother has a chronic disease that has all the siblings attempting to come to terms with the eventual death of our eighty-eight-year-old mother. We are accustomed to working together to reach consensus and support her life choices. I am grateful for my siblings who are willing to work together for the future realities when making decisions about our extended family.

Following my true nature, this path has filled me with gratitude, becoming even more resilient with change and loss. My heart is grateful for my journey. I know I have a choice every day to see our world as one of hope, or one of despair. I choose hope! This has been the only way for me to *Rise with Resilience!*

Carla Beckerle, DNP, APRN-BC, has over 40 years of experience in health care. During her years in the inpatient setting, she managed critical care, emergency, case management and utilization services. In the outpatient setting, she serves in the role of Vice President of Clinical Programs. This role includes strategic planning and oversight of the company's case management and wellness teams. She practices clinically on a regular basis and precepts nurse practitioner students during her clinical hours.

Beckerle earned her Doctor of Nursing Practice from St. Louis University School of Nursing in 2013 and is an adjunct professor at the University of Missouri St. Louis in the DNP nursing program. Beckerle is a member of the ADA, is a content expert reviewer for Diabetes Spectrum magazine, a member of NANDA International Expert Clinical Advisory Panel (ECAP), AANP/ANA/MONA St. Louis and State Chapters, STLNAP and AMNP St. Louis Chapters.

Family and friends are very precious to Carla and her motto in life is "let's try it." Piano, scrapbooking, boating, and travel help support her quest for joy. Throughout her life experiences, Carla learned that following her true nature with gratitude in her heart and head, hope in her heart, and optimism as her core value.

www.facebook.com/carla.beckerle
www.linkedin.com/in/carla-beckerle-2949328/
cbeckerle@essehealth.com

■

Rosalind (Roz) Norman, DMgt

Reimagining Our Communities

Building Bridges During the Pandemic

It's been said that we use our energy to build, not destroy. Since the advent of the recent pandemic, many of us have had to face unthinkable decisions about our collective health—health of ourselves, our families, our communities, our nation, and our world.

At first, it could seem that it's only about the individual. But it's bigger than that. When this virus became more apparent in various cities and towns across the United States of America, it became real. It was here and in our face. We could not escape it.

Personal Journey

Since I was eight years old, I wanted to help people. At that age, I proudly announced to my mother and stepfather that I wanted to be a missionary or nun.

Of course, I later realized that I can be a missionary in my own backyard—meaning where I grew up. Growing up during the 1960s in an inner-city war zone ridden with violence, drug abuse, and decimated neighborhoods, I had to learn how to navigate between downtown and midtown St. Louis, cope with racist and corrupt cops, maneuver around gangs who waged war over illegal drug distribution, yearn for families barely existing on minimum wages, and make the most of my public school's limited resources of equipment and outdated books for knowledge-starved students.

Although I became a single mother in 1973 while attending college, it has not been an easy path to accomplish what I sensed as my purpose. I didn't know then—I was learning to *Rise with Resilience.*

I certainly learned about resilience during that time of my life. I was not encouraged to pursue my love for the arts or the convergence of media and entertainment or emerging technologies. Even more so, I was ridiculed for my vision to see a connection between computer-driven technologies and a future unlike what was known at the time. However, since the 1970s, my volunteer contributions, as well as paid work, consisted of projects which relied on various technologies. I often developed and implemented programs, using these different technologies, to serve young people in communities similar to the one I lived in throughout my childhood to adulthood.

Discovering my abilities to organize various kinds of community-based events, to mobilize people to carry out tasks associated with different events, and to be innovative with mostly non-existing resources became tools in my repertoire to be of service in Communities of Color. Although born and raised in St. Louis, Missouri, I visited major cities such as Atlanta, Chicago, Kansas City, Las Vegas, Los Angeles, Washington, D.C., and the Bronx. I wanted to learn about best-practices in managing community-building initiatives.

At the same time, I continued my education in areas related to public affairs, mass communications, multi-cultural management, and organizational development. For post-graduate studies, I went to Regent's College (now Regent's University) in London, England. I spent a semester learning more about cross-cultural management plus organizational change and development.

Then, later in my mid-fifties, I completed a doctoral degree in management. By that time, I had obtained considerable experiences dealing with people from diverse backgrounds. I had learned how to conduct meetings with people one-on-one and in small group settings. It gave me insight about what I needed to do next.

Communities of Color Inequities

As a Black female, although I understood the distrust of the vaccine in my community, I decided to receive the vaccine and booster injection to combat the virus. Inasmuch, when considering the basis of distrust during this lingering pandemic, I recall how the ill-fated Tuskegee Experiment allowed Black men to be infected and die from complications associated with syphilis. It's finally part of public record as follows:

By the end of the study in 1972, only 74 of the test subjects were alive. Of the original 399 men, 28 had died of syphilis, 100 were dead of related complications, 40 of their wives had been infected, and 19 of their children were born with congenital syphilis.

Then, here in St. Louis, there was an experiment which involved residents of the Pruitt-Igoe housing complex during 1953-1954 and 1963-1965. It was revealed on September 29, 2012 in Clinical News (https://clinicalnews.org/2014/01/19/revealed-army-scientists-secretly-sprayed-st-louis-with-radioactive-particles-for-years-to-test-chemical-warfare-technology-2/amp/) that Army scientists secretly sprayed radioactive particles to test chemical warfare technology. I lived across from the housing complex during both time periods. Talking about People of Color having the ability to cope and bounce back after this kind of mistreatment, I lived and learned about *Rising with Resilience* in real time.

These examples of public health injustices remind me of a poignant poem "We Wear the Mask" by Paul Laurence Dunbar (1872-1906). It's relevant still today.

We Wear the Mask

We wear the mask that grins and lies,
It hides our cheeks and shades our eyes,
This debt we pay to human guile;
With torn and bleeding hearts we smile,
And mouth with myriad subtleties.

Why should the world be over-wise,
In counting all our tears and sighs?
Nay, let them only see us, while
We wear the mask.

We smile, but, O great Christ, our cries
To thee from tortured souls arise.
We sing, but oh the clay is vile
Beneath our feet, and long the mile;
But let the world dream otherwise,
We wear the mask!

GatewayGIS: Bridging Gaps

After conducting research for my next big project, now named GatewayGIS, I enlisted some people from St. Louis, Missouri and East St. Louis, Illinois, to engage with representatives of academia, government, industry, and nonprofit organizations. Our purpose was to provide guidance and support for an intermediary that focuses on social innovation. What drove this purpose was construction of the National Geospatial-Intelligence Agency West Headquarters in north St. Louis where I grew up.

Having a $1.7 billion federal complex built in my former neighborhood—a neighborhood neglected for the last several decades—became an impetus to act. So, after ten months of preparation with committed community partners, I launched GatewayGIS on May 23, 2019.

GatewayGIS is a social innovation intermediary that's run by skilled volunteers. As the architect of the intermediary, I recruit highly skilled volunteers who believe in "giving back" to the community as I do. We give freely of our time, talents, and resources. I purposely do not receive compensation for managing GatewayGIS. For me, it's paramount that I "walk the talk" by being forthright about my purpose.

The volunteers, who become collaborators, help me to connect individuals and organizations with resources to people without resources. GatewayGIS collaborators also provide a variety of services related to curriculum development and/or identification of specific kinds of curricula, free community workshops, paid and unpaid internships, mentoring, entrepreneurial joint ventures, and inclusion of a multiple generation learning environment. Through continuous learning, we are developing a community-building pipeline *From the Cradle to C-Suite and Beyond* to reinforce the need for early intervention and career education.

Starting in underserved, under-resourced communities in the St. Louis Region, GatewayGIS initially designed a tripartite model for daytime in schools, after school, and on Saturdays, to encourage job-readiness training for geospatial technology. More recently, because of efforts needed to prepare for the future of work happening now, GatewayGIS collaborators pivoted to integrate emerging technologies, such as artificial intelligence, machine learning, robotics, drone technology, augmented and virtual reality, the Internet of Things, blockchain technology, and 3D printing, along with geospatial technology.

When the pandemic was realized finally in March 2020, GatewayGIS collaborators and community stakeholders had to adjust quickly via the use of different online sources. Because Communities of Color were devastated beyond what had been revealed before the spread of this worldwide deadly virus, we devised plans to help GatewayGIS collaborators to refocus on the growing urgency for keeping our students, teachers, parents, and community advocates engaged and productive.

Our students daily faced death from the virus. Some of my family members were hospitalized and a couple of them died. Several of my friends lost loved ones, too.

Inasmuch, once vaccinations became available, many People of Color resisted the inoculations. At the same time, each day increasing numbers of People of Color were infected; many died needlessly due to distrust of the medical system.

For underserved, under-resourced Communities of Color to continue rising up and being resilient during the pandemic, more empathy and creative long-term solutions were needed. GatewayGIS collaborators realized how essential it was to get input and nurture relationships with students, parents, teachers, and community advocates, particularly in Communities of Color.

I believe the African and Asian proverb, "It takes a village to raise a child." And when it comes to GatewayGIS, I urge our collaborators to understand that People of Color have been traumatized long before the recent pandemic. By adding the adverse impact of this pandemic to an existing cycle of traumatic experiences, mental health services are needed too.

In other words, an integrated systemwide approach is needed to address the entire well-being of everyone, their family, and others within Communities of Color. And that's where GatewayGIS collaborators attempt to fill the gaps and bridge the digital, geographic, cultural, racial, and economic divisions, formed before and which continued throughout the pandemic. We expanded beyond the initial tripartite model and *THRIVED!*

Besides our virtual programs, such as the GatewayGIS Virtual Speakers Series, we formed alliances with widely respected education and research organizations to develop and implement a series of monthly traveling community workshops. These workshops would travel to underserved, under-resourced Communities of Color in Illinois, and Missouri. Our purpose in doing this is to share information about different emerging technologies and skills required for employment and entrepreneurial opportunities.

Instead of becoming paralyzed by fearing the negative impact of the pandemic on education, employment, and small business ownership, GatewayGIS increased its efforts to develop alliances, use different modes of communication, and create smaller sized sessions for community engagement. As Marvel movie character King T'Challa said in film *Black Panther* (2018), "We all know the truth….in times of crisis, the wise build bridges."

Lessons Learned

In support of *Rising with Resilience*, there are five lessons I learned from the pandemic:

1. Foremost, the importance of letting people know you care—you care about them and their struggles for survival.

2. Second, I must "walk the talk" and be authentically me. I must live what I say that I'm going to do. I must be a walking double-sided billboard that describes what I'm trying to do. Then, do all I can to make it happen. So many underserved and under-resourced individuals, who I serve, crave for people to truthfully do what they say they're going to do. If that means I'll meet with you and share a meal, then I must keep my word. Words mean nothing without action to follow up on them.

3. Third, recruit skilled volunteers, whose beliefs and philosophies align. For me, it's compassion in action to freely give of your time, talents, and resources to individuals of lesser chance and who do not have adequate resources to live, work, and thrive. So, I look for skilled volunteers who are willing to give back and

freely provide their time, talents, and resources as I do.

4. Fourth, with the help of mentors throughout my life, I've learned to meet people where they are. I cannot expect to nurture a relationship without taking time to listen, observe, and learn about individuals who I want to serve and how to help them. I must suspend a temptation to have preconceived notions about what I think about individuals who might look different than I do... who might talk different than I do...who might hold different opinions than I do.

5. Lastly, I know what I do is bigger than me. But I also know that there's power when one person takes a stand to do what is true, noble, right, pure, and lovely. For reimagining our communities, it starts with one person imagining how they can do something to uplift another person who's in pain or suffering or oppressed with the inequities of today's flawed society and human-caused divisions.

This is *Rising with Resilience.*

Since 1971, Rosalind (Roz) Norman, DMgt, also known affectionately as "Dr. Roz", collaborates with various stakeholders from academia, government, industry, and community nonprofit organizations to develop and implement innovative initiatives for underserved, under-resourced youth and their communities in Illinois and Missouri.

Roz serves on the frontline as an advocate for STEAM (Science, Technology, Engineering, Arts, and Mathematics) career education and served as the Eastern Region Co-Chair for the Missouri Statewide Task Force on African American Issues in Mental Health. By freely giving back of her time, talents, and resources, she fulfills a tenet for what she does.

She obtained a Doctor of Management degree from the School of Business and Technology at Webster University in St. Louis, Missouri. Check out her latest projects, co-developed with young people and adult collaborators for GatewayGIS, via www.gatewaygis.org.

www.facebook.com/Gateway-GIS-2304212626295922
www.linkedin.com/in/gateway-gis-187151182/
www.twitter.com/GatewayGIS and www.twitter.com/DrRozNor

■

Julie Irwin, MSN, FNP-BC

Life-Changing Moments

Have you ever had that one defining moment, that moment where the domino representing your life's path is tipped and starts to fall, forever changing the course of your life? Mine is still clear as a cloudless blue sky, thirty-two years later. My path abruptly changed course on what should have been a normal Thursday at 10:55 a.m.—the time of the accident. One hour and thirty-five minutes later, at 12:30 p.m., that life-altering moment took place, called out as the "event finale"; the time of death.

I was eight years old, extremely shy and introverted, running barefoot and wild outside, completely obsessed with horses from my earliest memory. My dad worked at a coffee delivery company just across the state line and my mother was a school bus driver. The small-town school and bus garage was just down the hill from our small, old farmhouse. My parents were regular church-goers, and every Saturday my parents and the four siblings would pack into our beat up, old car and head to church.

"Saturday?" you say; yes, Saturday. My parents' faith was part of a rather Old-Testament belief system. It was a day of rest from Friday evening to Saturday evening, so no Saturday morning cartoons—ever. No celebration of birthdays or other "pagan" holidays, such as Christmas or Easter, and definitely no Halloween! It was a belief system that didn't quite mix with traditional medicine either. If you were sick, a minister would come to your home and anoint you, praying for your recovery. No doctors, no vaccinations. We were taught only those in our faith would be allowed into "God's Kingdom."

As a child, the only thing I liked about church was knowing, on the Friday night before, we might get a candy treat. I don't remember ever questioning why only those in our church would be allowed into God's Kingdom, but I did question the fact that animals wouldn't be there. More specifically, horses. I just could not imagine experiencing eternal life after death in a place where horses had no existence. Why would God not give eternal life after death to all his creations?

My parents always claimed to like animals, but you can always tell by someone's interaction with pets just how much they value the idea that animals have their own spirit and soul. Children are even more astute at this observation. The day I officially labeled church and religion as a sham was the day we had to leave a kitten to die because it was time to go to church—there would be no exception. The kitten had fallen out of a milk crate, which was sitting on a dusty shelf in our old detached garage, right into a puddle of oil on the dirty floor beneath it. Instead of caring for one of God's creatures on this church day, we had to leave it, covered in oil, to die.

Although my disdain for church and religion has remained constant since that day, my spirituality and faith in God has also always remained constant and has always been an integral part of my Rising. I never blamed God for the faulty thoughts and actions of man.

I would think if you polled all children in every household, they would say they had a favorite parent or a parent that they connected with more. For me, and likely for all my siblings, that was my dad. He was a handsome guy and people always told him he looked like Superman or Tom Cruise. More than that, he was kind, generous, and forgiving. He was that guy that set up a field trip for elderly people without transportation to come to our house and pick veggies out of the vegetable garden to take back to the nursing home. He always wanted to help people and had wanted to go to school for speech therapy. He was always the parent that had time for us when he wasn't at work. When I got into trouble, like children usually do, and it was his turn to be the parent and punish me, he would just take me into my bedroom, sit me down, and talk to me in a very calm voice about what I did wrong. No belts, paddles, or boards necessary. This always resonated with me as a more effective alternative to the authoritarian style of my mother. And memories of children are long.

On that Thursday afternoon, December 28th, 1989, I was sitting in our kitchen while my mother was doing her usual kitchen duties. The old-time yellow rotary dial phone hanging on the kitchen wall rang. I don't know how I knew, but I did. I said something out loud to the effect of "That's about Dad. He's hurt." The look of my mother's face and her reaction after answering the phone seemed expected to me, rather than alarming. She looked panicked and in tears.

Someone she knew eventually came to pick us up and take us to an emergency department in an old hospital in St. Louis, one that doesn't even exist anymore. I remember walking down a long empty hallway lined with doors to one side. We eventually stopped at one of those doors and waited. A lady dressed in scrubs came out and started talking with my mother. The lady looked at me and then back at my mother, stating she didn't think I should be allowed into the room, hinting at the unpleasant sight within. That's really all I remember from that day, but it's a memory I will never forget. My siblings and I were later told by my mom and the family that my dad was no longer with us and that he had "died instantly from a broken neck." I don't know why but I always knew this wasn't the whole truth. I never had closure because I was never given a chance to have closure. That was my first experience coming into contact with the medical field, or even knowing it existed for that matter.

Life threw a lot of curve balls at me after that day, including losing the home we had shared with Dad to a hundred-year flood, just three years later; living in a place nicknamed "FEMA-ville," full of FEMA trailers, like the name implies; going through an extreme period of depression, hopelessness, and suicidal thoughts as an eleven-year-old child; moving out onto my own when I was sixteen; surfing from one couch to another like a vagrant; fighting poverty and struggling to better myself. Through all of this, I never lost faith in God and I always focused on my blessings. I focused on someday still attaining my dream of having a horse. And I never stopped wanting the truth about what happened to my dad all those years ago.

What was that day like for Dad? I know that he was doing a late morning delivery in his work van, slowly cruising along in the far-right lane. In a split second, a car coming from the opposite direction veered into his lane, hitting him head on, causing his van to be thrown off to the side of the road from the sheer force of the collision. The space where he was sitting crumpled like a soda can—steering wheel almost pushing into the back of his chair, his chest caught in the middle. He was still alive and fighting for his life when he arrived at the emergency department at 11:29 a.m., surviving for another sixty-one minutes until he was pronounced dead at 12:30 p.m., various tubes and needles puncturing his body, but unable to be saved due to severe bleeding in his brain, heart, and lungs.

The twenty-year-old driver that hit my dad's van swerved across four lanes of traffic, missing two other cars in order to reach my dad, almost like it was predestined.

I think about these events of my life on a fairly regular basis, always wondering what life might have looked like if I had lived a normal childhood. Wishing I would have had a chance to ask him why he believed in the church the way he did or why he made some of the decisions he made. I've come to the conclusion that no one is perfect, everybody makes mistakes or choices they may later regret. This is being human. Life is what you make it; and the harder the life, the greater the potential for growth and reflection. Some get stuck blaming the past, romancing what could have been; others use the past to create a better future. I have chosen to do the latter. That old hospital where my dad died became part of the university campus where I would later receive both my bachelor's and master's degrees of nursing.

If I could tell Dad one thing, it would be to say thank you. Thank you for your sacrifice, providing me with resilience and purpose.

This was my Rising to becoming an emergency medicine nurse practitioner.

Julie Irwin is an emergency medicine nurse practitioner at a busy trauma hospital in St. Louis, Missouri. She received both her bachelor's and master's degrees from University of Missouri-St. Louis. She spent eight years working as an emergency department RN prior to becoming a nurse practitioner.

Julie and her significant other, Roberto, enjoy the country life together on their small hobby farm in Wildwood, Missouri, with her two amazing horses, Carmel and Daazi, as well as their spoiled canine, Zelda.

Carmel is a twenty-one-years young Foxtrotter that has been with Julie for fourteen years. Julie adopted Daazi, a seven-year-old Mustang, almost two years ago from the Extreme Mustang Challenge, an event bringing awareness for wild mustangs needing homes. Julie and Roberto adopted Zelda from a city shelter last year; and although she had a pretty rough life before her rescue, she has settled right into this thing called "love."

equinelvr10@yahoo.com

■

Robin L. Owens, Ph.D.

"Who Do You Want to Be?"

"Don't make it bigger than what it is, Sis." These are the words that my brother spoke to me about a year before the CDC determined that we were in a world health crisis. At the time my brother said this to me, I had no idea that they would become some of the last words he would speak to me. It was during one of our regular Sunday afternoon phone conversations as we shared about our respective weeks. He asked me, "how are you doing? I said, "mostly good and I'm feeling the pressure and overwhelm of an upcoming due date on a major project I'm working on." He didn't ask any questions about the project. He merely said in a caring and calming voice, "don't make it bigger than what it is, Sis." Immediately, I felt a sense of relief because I realized that I was doing just that—making it bigger that what it was. Fast forward to a little over a year later and my brother had been told by doctors that he had six months left to live. He received the diagnosis in the Spring and in the Fall, he was gone.

During those last months, he remained steady, graceful, and kind. We were fortunate enough to have many heartfelt conversations during that time. As I reflect back now, I'm struck by how his words, "Don't make it bigger than what it is," have become a guiding light for me long after his death, especially during that dreadful week when the CDC determined that we were in the midst of a global health crisis.

Like almost everyone else, I was in a complete panic. I didn't know what to do. I didn't know how to even think about what was going on.

We had not experienced anything like this in our lifetimes. At first, I kept asking myself, "what are you going to do?" Then I heard someone else mention that they were going to focus on *who they want to be* when the crisis was over. That struck a chord in my heart and soul, so I adopted it. I changed my question from, "What are you going to do?" to "Who do you want to be when this is over?" Asking that new question set me on a path that helped me to rise with resilience throughout the pandemic.

Guided By a New Question

Who do I want to be when this is over? I had a new question. How did I begin to answer it? I took some time away from the news reports, social media, and conversations with others to just be quiet. During that time, I suddenly remember my brothers' words, "Don't make it bigger than what it is." Then I thought to myself, this global health crisis is BIG. There's no doubt about that. As I continued in silence, I took some time to reflect on what my brothers' words really meant to me. I came to understand that "it" did not refer merely to the situation, "it" referred to my response to the situation. Just as it was during my conversation with him about being stressed out and overwhelmed, so as it was in the case of the global health crisis, my response stemmed out of fear. In essence, he told me, "Don't let that fear have power over you."

Of course, fear is a natural response in this case. However, I had been allowing my thoughts, my actions, and my behaviors to be led by fear. Fear had been taking the lead in my life. The words, "Don't make it bigger than what it is," began to mean to me, "Don't let the fear have power over you. Don't let it keep you from moving forward." At the time of the conversation with my brother, fear showed up as stress, overwhelm, and overthinking, to name a few ways. During the first weeks of the global health crisis, fear showed up as focused on, "What am I going to do?" That question represented a fear of loss of control. It suggested that I could actually do something to control something that would make the whole situation bearable. Of course, there was nothing I could do to control things. What I could do instead was control my response to the situation and not let the fear take the drivers' seat.

The fear continued to vie for the leading role in my life. During that time, fear was raging everywhere. It was raging locally, nationally, and globally. Collectively, we were thinking about death because of the massive numbers of deaths that were happening all around us. That fear penetrated into my own mind. I thought to myself, "I must do something different. I can't keep focusing on this," yet I would watch the news to get caught up with what was happening on that day.

Shortly after the country went into the shelter in place mode, there were many social issues raised such as the painstaking experience of the death of George Floyd, which marked a defining moment in our history. Our collective consciousness was raised around those issues. Like many others, I felt enraged. Also, I felt a sense of being fearful about my own life. I thought about the extremists. On every side, there are extremists and the ones who were enacting this kind of violence could be anywhere. They could be in my neighborhood, they could be in my city, they could be wherever I am out and about around town. That thinking crept into my mind and I had fear because of that. I had fear of death from the pandemic. Added to that, I had fear about the possibility of death as a result of encountering some outraged extremist. Fear was prevalent in my thinking, just as it was with many others.

Led by Purpose, Not Fear

In the midst of all the fear, I knew that I did not want it to have power over me. I went back to spending some time in quiet. There, I was reminded of the question, "Who do I want to be when this health crisis is over?" The answer began to emerge. I didn't want to be a person who was led by fear. I wanted to be a person who was led by purpose. So, I asked myself, "What's something you've been yearning to do that you felt as if you haven't had time, energy, or wherewithal to attend to?" Then it occurred to me that for well over a year before the start of the pandemic, I had been wanting to start a podcast. It felt like it would be a way to serve my long-held mission to support high-achieving women and add to my sense of purpose. However, I had been letting fear hold me back from doing it. The fear was under the guise of "I don't know how to do it" and "I don't have time to do it" and "I don't this…" and "I don't that…"

With my renewed focus on being led by purpose and on not letting fear have power over me, I wondered whether starting a podcast would be in alignment with my purpose or not. To help me make the decision, I turned to the Purpose-Based, Decision-Making System that I created a few years earlier and had been teaching high-achieving women to use. The system is designed for you to ask yourself four questions. If the answer is yes to all four questions, then that's an indicator that you are making a decision that is in alignment with your purpose. The questions are:

1. Does this involve something I really love?

2. Does this involve something that really matters to me?

3. Does this allow me to use one or more of my natural abilities?

4. Does this involve serving something or someone beyond myself?

I asked myself all four questions about starting the podcast. The answer was yes to all of them! I decided that I was going to start a podcast even in the midst of all that was going on or especially because of all that was going on. Although I didn't know how, I made the decision anyway. Then about two weeks later, just like that, someone popped into my life through social media who happened to be a podcast manager. She asked, "Does anyone need help with starting a podcast?" I said, "Yes!" We connected with each other and started the podcast. It is still going today and it plays an important role in helping me to fulfill my life's mission and sense of purpose, as well as helping high-achieving women, and those aspiring to be led by purpose.

The lesson I learned from all of this is that I did not let the fear of the pandemic that was swirling around lead my thoughts, behaviors, and actions. I let purpose—disguised in a combination of my passions, values, natural abilities, and service—lead the way. The focus on my desire to be a person who is led by purpose guided me to make a Purpose-Based Decision which in turn serves an important part of my life's mission. As a result, the greater sense of purpose and mission helped me to rise with resilience during a time of tremendous crisis. I hope this reflection on my personal experience encourages, inspires, and motivates you to make Purpose-Based Decisions and rise with resilience during challenging times or times of crisis.

Robin L. Owens, Ph.D. is a tenured college professor in the Religious Studies Department at Mount Saint Mary's University in Los Angeles. There she teaches, inspires, and motivates aspiring women leaders to pursue meaning and purpose.

Outside of the classroom Robin spends her time fulfilling her mission to support high-achieving women leaders. In service to her mission, she is the host of the popular podcast "Leadership Purpose with Dr. Robin;" CEO and Founder of the training company, MASTERFUL Course Creations, LLC, and author of two upcoming books, *"Making Purpose-Based Decisions: An Inspirational Guide to More Meaning and Purpose in Your Business or Career,"* and *"My Faith in the Constitution is Whole: Barbara Jordan and the Politics of Scripture"* which is about the unique way Barbara Jordan lived out her leadership purpose.

When she is not working, she is walking in the park, laughing with friends, or delighting over the fact that she convinced her nieces and nephews that she's the cool aunt.

www.linkedin.com/in/robinlowensphd
www.RobinLOwens.com
www.CreateMASTERFULCourses.com
www.podcasts.apple.com/us/podcast/leadership-purpose-with-dr-robin/id1552322410

■

Janet N. Haas, BSN, RN

Here and There

I fell into nursing. Really, I did. When choosing what course of study to take in college, nursing wasn't on my mind specifically, but I thought something medical. I had experience with the medical field, having been born with cleft palate. Hospitals and doctors' offices were comfortable places. Teaching was an option, too. I had spent junior high explaining theorems to my fellow classmates as they turned to me to explain what the teacher had just said. Maybe teaching was my forte. With those possibilities, my initial major was "undecided."

That first semester, an acquaintance in the college dorm asked me if I wanted to attend the School of Nursing program's application presentation the following evening. I did. Listening to the presentation, it struck me that the field of nursing blended both my familiarity of the medical environment and the joy of teaching. The variety of settings requiring a nurse appealed to me, too. I was no longer undecided! Nursing was what I wanted to do as my vocation. I was accepted into the program, graduated, and received licensure. In nursing school, the instructors discussed the importance of advancing beyond my bachelor's degree. I thought, "*I want to be hands-on, improving patient outcomes. Why do I need a masters? Let me use this degree first!*

While in college, I met my husband. He was in ROTC, expecting to make the military his career. Fast-forward, and together, we have moved every one-to-two-years, living on both coasts and cities in-between.

Wherever he was stationed, I found positions in skilled nursing facilities or med-surg/oncology units.

Those positions fit my personality and were readily available.

I realized my husband and I would never be in one place long enough to complete a master's program, nor that I'd need one as my stop/start career continued no matter where we lived. That was okay for me. I was able to use the last job to get the next. The skilled nursing facility (SNF) Charge Nurse position was the steppingstone for the med/surg position, and so forth. Once, had we not moved, I would have been offered my ideal position in the employee education department. At heart, I am that teacher from childhood, wanting to impart the understanding of "why" we take the actions we do. Over the years, having staff verbalize appreciation of my quick, on-the-spot teaching moments is gratification enough. Our chosen lifestyle challenged me to rise with resilience, continue my career, no matter where we lived.

As additional children came along and our family grew, part-time work was best for my psyche with the added demands of homelife. My day off gave me the energy to get everything done. More importantly, when my husband was on ship tour, I would play the role of being the single parent and would stay home and not work. We didn't have the backup network of family to help with emergencies or enjoy hospital work-hours conducive with daycare centers' hours of operation. Even shore positions can be demanding on the service member's time and energy. What should be considered family time can get shoved aside as national/global crises arise and sometimes can require reminding the service member they need to find the energy to attend children's school functions or sporting events to give them memories of both parents watching their life moments. No matter what, we were committed to the decision that I would work every shore duty to stay current and practice my degree. Besides, I loved nursing. Helping people came natural for me.

Although, as I have gotten older, incorporating a part-time job each time my husband came home for shore duty, coupled with the added demands of my already tapped-out time and energy, caused periods of anxiousness. I can't deny my drive to use my education—I like the work and tasks of nursing. Superiors validate my contributions to patient care and outcomes; patients/families appreciate the explanations and reasons for the care provided. But it's not easy and nurses can develop stress symptoms too. Once, while needing to work through a looming, personal family decision, I developed bigeminy—but like magic, the irregular heartbeats disappeared once I finalized the decision.

Committed to career advancement, my husband returned for one last ship duty. But unlike the past, I decided to keep my current job, as telecommuting was available in my utilization review position. I was convinced I could make it work while he was on a ship tour—that is, be responsible for house and kids by myself—which broke our rule that worked for us, of me staying home while he was gone. Then, I broke the other rule: increasing to full time and losing my day off. Still, I was thinking, *"I can do this!"*

I had managed (barely) through the initial eight months of my husband's return to ship duty. Then, came the additional six months of him being deployed at sea. The stress of life became overwhelming ... I plowed through insomnia ... then eye-twitching. Not until I developed a sensation of cutting, did I realize I had no choice. I needed to resign. Initially, I felt defeated, but my improved psyche determined that the decision I made was best for me, for the family.

Looking back, I see myself *Rising with Resilience* no matter what life throws at me. I learned from each experience, and I learned to recognize and accept my mental limits. My husband had two shore-duty positions after that last ship tour. I didn't work during either. The remote location would have required a long commute; and my aging parents needed my attention. Family was more important than sustaining a career.

When life became calmer, I chose to work at rehab/SNF, wanting a slower pace and to know the residents in my care. I've also been able to do those teaching moments with staff and residents. Working gives me joy. My nursing and life experience is appreciated.

Now, having worked past those darkest days of the pandemic, donning new PPE between SNF residents, I still wonder, "*Will I catch this ever-changing virus?*" We've lost dear residents, causing sadness. Though, by my knowledge and care, I can comfort family and give the resident a peaceful close to their life.

As the nursing shortage continues, it's rare to end a shift on time. Personally, the feelings of being overwhelmed came back. The insomnia and eye-twitching returned. Anxiety impacts the needed clarity of thought to give the utmost care to those in your charge. I realized that I can't fill every hole in the schedule, but I can work the shifts that make the most impact. For me, the awareness and need for self-preservation won! I cut back on my availability. A healthy me is paramount for everyone.

My tip for you: Understanding your limits is just as important as realizing your strengths.

Janet is a proud graduate of the University of Missouri, Columbia Sinclair School of Nursing. She and her husband settled in the Madison, Wisconsin, area after he completed his seventeenth tour of duty. No longer vagabonds, Janet has been able to volunteer for church committees, expand their home's flower gardens, and sew oodles of baby blankets and bibs for friends and family.

M I Z ... Z O U (Sorry. It's an MU expression).

haasjanet78@gmail.com

■

Michelle Burk, DNP, WHNP-BC

A PASSION FOR RESILIENCE

My passion for women's health started after I graduated from nursing school. I started my career in St. Louis as a nurse working with moms during pregnancy and the postpartum period. The latter evolved my love for women's health and introduced me to the idea of continuing with schooling as a Nurse Practitioner. Now that I've been in practice as a Women's Health Nurse Practitioner for more than 16 years, I can honestly say I will retire with this career. I have found my niche! I am thankful for all the females who have allowed me to care for them over the years. I have built a network of friends and community from this amazing career!

My role in women's health has helped me become a better person not only taking care of patients but taking care of myself and my children. I work full time, watch my children's sports, fit in exercise daily and other aspects of life. I continue to grow and teach other females daily that "WE COME FIRST!" We need to put ourselves first, as well as help each other through the amusing story of life. The empowerment that we can have as females in our daily profession, but by teaching our young girls that we can *Rise with Resilience* to do what we put our minds to, in any daily task or life goal. When I see females in the office, whether young or older, it is my job to make sure they are fully aware they can fit in time for themselves. To be a better mom, wife, friend, caregiver we need to take the time to better ourselves as well. I use exercise to help with the health of my body physically but also for my mental health and stress reduction.

I teach my girls daily that we can do anything we put our minds to. In our house we have the motto of "GIRL POWER!" My 10-year- old son unfortunately must deal with his 2 teenage sisters and a mom who believes that females can run the world. Hopefully he will learn to treat females with respect. A large part of my mission taking care of my female patients is reminding them that we are all human and can *Rise with Resilience* when the days feel overwhelming. Personal growth is hard. Every human can benefit from personal growth. We are amazing individuals and deserve only the best for ourselves. We can Rise with Resilience from our past and should move on from whatever that may be. All of us have a story to tell and I will gladly share mine with whomever would like to listen.

This ever-changing world has brought new concepts and fears to healthcare. At the start of the pandemic, I got to see first-hand how pregnancy and deliveries were affected. My office opened a clinic just for pregnant females diagnosed with the virus. I saw these women weekly and had to dress in my lovely "space suit" to protect myself and others. When the day ended…the very second, I walked into the garage I had to change and then shower so I wouldn't spread germs. The idea of this virus at the time was scary for all. The inkling of catching this and bringing it home to my family was terrifying since it was all so unknown in the beginning.

While others got to work from home, in healthcare I went to work and took care of patients with the virus! The virus was mysterious to healthcare. Patients were scared as well, and can you imagine the stress the pregnant women felt?! At times, some of my friends and family members didn't want to be around me because I worked in healthcare, in fear of catching the virus.

■ ■ ■ ■ ■

Now in 2022 with the vaccine and new mandates, we do feel a more comfortable, but the virus is still affecting us and our patients. We have educated our patients as best we can in the healthcare community, helping them understand how to protect themselves and stay healthy. As a women's healthcare provider, I have learned to *Rise with Resilience* through this pandemic! In my world, being a provider, mom, and friend, I have learned to take each day as a new day. This pandemic has shown me such sorrow, and yet at the same time shown me to appreciate my life and not look far into the future as I am ever changing and growing.

Michelle Burk, DNP, is a board-certified women's health nurse practitioner. As a women's health nurse practitioner for BJC medical group, Michelle provides general obstetrics and gynecological care for her patients. She obtained her Doctorate of Nursing practice from the University of Missouri St. Louis. Outside of work, she enjoys spending time with her children whether at home or sports as well as any outdoor activity, mostly running.

www.linkedin.com/in/michelle-forseter-burk-dnp-whnp-bc-41102754/

■

Patrick Sherlock

The Silver Lining

As far back as I remember I always wanted to help people. In fact, I wanted to be a pediatrician since kindergarten. Certain events of my life brought me to where I am today, but never did I think I would be a healthcare provider in an age of a pandemic. But here I am. Patients and their family members often ask me the question, "How do you do this, day-in and day-out during a pandemic?" Opportunity exists in every situation where some doors will close but others will open. There is a silver lining in everything, even in the most volatile periods of humanity. We must see it and then seize the opportunity.

It was my freshmen year of high school when my world came crashing down after my mother was diagnosed with breast cancer. Thanks to modern day medicine and her healthcare team, she is here today getting to play with her grandchildren. Witnessing firsthand the medical and nursing care she received further sparked my interest in healthcare.

My junior year of high school we received a phone call about my brother being involved in a motor vehicle accident. He was ejected from the vehicle, shattering his pelvis and sustaining multiple injuries. I remember being in the ER trauma bay and watching medical personnel working together to achieve one common goal: saving his life. He was almost paralyzed from the waist down, and luckily his spinal cord was spared. He had a long road ahead of him, forcing him to move back home from college for physical rehabilitation. I had the opportunity to experience home health nursing and physical therapy which further reinforced my desire for a healthcare profession.

My uncle, a general surgeon, urged me to not become a physician but to go to nursing school and become a nurse practitioner. He navigated me through the process of becoming a registered nurse and later a nurse practitioner while assuring me the option to pursue medical school would remain on the table. During my sophomore year in high school, my anatomy teacher, a retired physician himself, would always speak highly of the nurse practitioner profession. At this point, I figured two physicians could not be wrong, so perhaps going to nursing school would be in my best interest. There were too many signs and too many people drawing me towards the nursing profession and so began my academic conquest.

I attended Texas Tech University Health Sciences Center in Lubbock Texas where I earned my bachelor's degree in nursing. There was a high demand for nurses in the Dallas-Ft. Worth Texas area, and following graduation, I relocated there.

I had bad test anxiety and subsequently failed nursing boards the first time, putting me on a different work schedule. I still had medical school on my radar until my life changed again when I met a girl on a hospital elevator named Katherine. Eventually I took my boards, passing them with flying colors, but if it were not for the schedule change, I might not have met my future wife.

Around this same time that I met Katherine, I had a month-long backpacking trip planned throughout Africa and to climb Mt. Kilimanjaro. Perhaps it was the limited oxygen or sheer exhaustion, but upon taking the summit I recall thinking that if she was still around when I got back, I was going to marry her. Exiting the airport, there she was waiting for me at the baggage claim! At that point I knew I wanted a family, without any burden of medical school.

By the age of 23 I travelled to several different countries, lived in Singapore, took the summit of mountain peaks, and swam in various oceans and seas. I was happy where I was with my accomplishments and pursuing a medical degree was no longer my priority. Katherine always pushed me to do more, as she knew bedside nursing was a stepping-stone for me. We attempted travel nursing but fell short when the 2008 recession occurred. So, we turned back to Dallas-Ft. Worth, landing us at Methodist Mansfield Medical Center.

Methodist Mansfield was a much smaller facility at that time, with only a six bed ICU. Coming from a much larger teaching hospital in the city to a small community-based suburban hospital was huge change for me. I found out quickly the resources I had at the bigger facility were nonexistent in this smaller facility, so being at the top of advanced cardiac life support skills was crucial.

One evening there were only two of us staffing the ICU. We had one patient coming from ER requiring emergent dialysis while another patient began declining, and a third patient was having profuse diarrhea. After several times of coding one patient and cleaning the backside of another patient throughout the night, I realized I had enough, and applied to graduate school the next day!

I did not get accepted into graduate school the first or second time I applied, but was later accepted into a nurse practitioner program at the University of Texas at El Paso. My training involved hospital medicine and critical care in the Dallas-Ft. Worth area where I was later recruited by a hospitalist group. It was at this time I was still transitioning out of my bedside role into the nurse practitioner role, yet it always seemed artificial, for some reason that I could not determine. Then one day, my attending physician was grilling me about a patient scenario where I did not step out of the nursing role. She said, "Patrick, work as team but understand you are no longer one of them, you are one of us, so act like it." So began the point of no return and my career as a nurse practitioner.

I did not have much appreciation for the business of healthcare at this point. In fact, my main goal was just to keep my patients alive. One of my patients, a retired trauma surgeon requiring back surgery, told me something I will never forget. He said, "Patrick, medicine is a very unforgiving profession." I asked him, "How so?" and he replied, "Because it will take you thousands of lives to save in order to consider yourself a legitimate provider, but it will only take one for it to all come crashing down."

His comment resonated with me and still does today. I knew I had to refine my skills but to also protect myself, so I studied more and attended conferences becoming more in tune with my profession. Around the same time another nurse practitioner and I opened an independent transitional care clinic which is where I had a newfound respect for the business and power of the healthcare industry. I figured pursuing my doctorate in nursing practice would solidify my new interest and give me the necessary knowledge to navigate through healthcare and run a successful business. I attended the University of Texas at Medical Branch in Galveston where I met important figures in academia who gave me those tools to succeed.

The clinic later proved to be financially harder than projected and could not be sustained, but the model worked and caught the attention of physicians in the community. I was later recruited by an internal medicine group to implement the model in their clinic and manage their inpatient population. The practice owner, who became my mentor and good friend today, recruited me at the time I was a hospitalist nurse practitioner. He said, "You have the mindset that will outgrow this position and you cannot be here forever." I asked if he could show me different. His response, "Take a leap of faith and I will show you."

I joined a robust internal medicine private practice in Dallas-Ft. Worth, Texas and became faculty at Texas Wesleyan University. I learned to maximize the hours of the day and learned to work smarter, not harder. I thought I was at the height of my career, and then the pandemic struck. I was let go from my faculty position for financial reasons, but I knew I wanted to continue pursuing academia. I later accepted a position at

DeSales University in Center Valley, Pennsylvania, being offered director-ship for the adult geriatric acute care nurse practitioner program.

Many ask how I live in Texas and direct a program in Pennsylvania during the rise of the pandemic. Doors closed for me, but others opened. Some options were right, but others were wrong. I did not look at the wrong door as failure, but rather something to learn from. I learned to maximize 24 hours in a day, and to compromise nowhere. Equally important, I learned to see the silver lining even in the direst circumstances. At the end of day, my secret to success and resilience came through my own tragedies, my love, failures of my own, wisdom of others, and taking a leap of faith.

Patrick J. Sherlock is a doctoral prepared acute care nurse practitioner holding licensure in Texas and Pennsylvania. He is currently a provider with Mansfield Medical Associates within the Dallas-Fort Worth, Texas metropolitan area with privileges at Methodist Mansfield Medical Center. He serves as Program Director for the Adult Geriatric Acute Care Nurse Practitioner program at DeSales University in Center Valley, Pennsylvania.

He shares his time between his Texas practice and academic responsibilities in Pennsylvania. He is an expert panelist chair for the ANCC board certification and preceptor for AGACNP students. He is a member of various organizations and was inducted into The Honor Society of Phi Kappa Phi, Sigma Theta Tau International Honor Society of Nursing & Golden Key Honor Society. His residence is Mansfield, Texas where he lives with his wife, Katherine and two children, Alexander and Emmerson. His personal interests are traveling and lounging with his family.

www.facebook.com/profile.php?id=16719604.

www.linkedin.com/in/patrick-sherlock-dnp-aprn-agacnp-bc-947339137/

■

Dr. Jessica Giddens

Resilience with Vision of the Future: My Story

As a nurse for thirteen years, specializing in complex medical psychiatric cases and integrative psychiatry, I've noted that our healthcare system requires a metamorphosis. Hope Advocacy can incite the change our broken healthcare system demands. Hope Advocacy sounds like a fabricated term pasted on a board to motivate nurses. *I can assure you, Hope Advocacy is a term that should inspire action in every nurse practicing today.* Hope Advocacy has been instrumental since the inception of my practice in 2013—especially during the recent pandemic. Hope, the cornerstone of resilience, is an optimistic state of mind that believes in positive outcomes. Advocacy is defined by action, and Hope Advocacy is delivering an optimistic state of mind through action.

Like most children, I didn't originally choose nursing, but dreamt of other careers; a stark contrast to the dreams of my children: "YouTuber, computer programmer, and my four-year-old daughter declares "Princess Elsa." I aspired towards STEM careers until some misogynist chemistry teacher left me feeling too stupid for science. I tried my hand in many non-STEM fields but wanted so badly to find a career where my hard work meant something! *Healthcare it was!* The career change at that moment in my life might have been the hallmark of my epic social idealist stupidity right there. Bless my social ethical idealist heart!

I chose nursing over medical school because I wanted to be a mom. I thought nursing was the better option to juggle medical goals with reduced education expenses and motherhood. By the time I was through my APRN degree, I thought owning my own business would perfectly capture the work-life balance I desired for nursing and motherhood.

I managed a master's program, doctorate program, clinicals, and working, while still managing three pregnancies, and being a mom and wife. I spent six years building my practice. Given my autism, I obsessively studied, and researched, becoming the best integrative psychiatric APRN in the area while juggling motherhood and my own business. I rotated more than 100 students a year and spoke nationally. Sometimes there wasn't enough of me to see the patients in between the onslaught of speaking engagements, key opinion leader meetings, conferences, and pharmaceutical advisory boards on multiple drug products, genomics, and disease states. There certainly wasn't enough of me at home, despite the original work-life balance goals I'd set for myself. At work, I prided myself on being different, diverging from my medically trained algorithmic care model, opting for a unique blend of pharmacogenomics, holistic and complementary medicine.

One favorite quote that I always felt resonated with my practice style is by Clara Barton: "I have an almost complete disregard of precedent and a faith in the possibility of something better. It irritates me to be told how things always have been done ... I defy the tyranny of precedent. I cannot afford the luxury of a closed mind. I go for anything new that might improve the past." Barton's quote exemplifies my spirit in nursing.

Patients gravitated toward my unorthodox approach. They came to me saying, "Jessica, you are my last hope, my plan truly is suicide if you can't help me"; most just bereft in a system failing them. They required personalized medicine an operationally inefficient system refused to provide. My healthcare algorithms were my own, avoiding cumbersome processes and ineffective care management.

Before discovering my practice, some patients spent 20-40 plus years drifting from doctor to doctor. Most were begging for more than a 5-minute consult and script. Inflammation and complex medical and neuropsychiatric conditions defined the basis of many of their symptoms rather than the stigmatizing and oppressive psychiatric labels. A barrage of misdiagnosed patients entered my practice: females with cancer accused of anorexia nervosa; women with autoimmune conditions merely labeled "psychosomatic;" patients with complex seizures labeled with "pseudo-seizures;" and autism spectrum disorder marginalized by a myriad of axis II personality disorders. I don't believe in somatization disorders, nor do I have any love for the DSM which offers nebulous diagnoses, ignoring neuroscience-based nomenclature and the principles of physical medicine.

In 2019 and 2020, the exact time I started as the CEO of my own Holocracy nurse practitioner business, Holon Inclusive Healthcare, the next wave of stress hit with the onset of the pandemic. But my patients were solid. With an array of individualized treatments, my patients stayed out of the hospital. They were all doing great, for a while... Virus wave after virus wave. I watched the insidious deterioration as patients started getting care less than inadequate. The already broken system was crumbling into a wasteland of healthcare devastation and trauma. I too was hit with the virus. I started fighting alongside my patients to get medical attention while family watched helplessly as my health rapidly declined.

Post-traumatic stress disorder swelled in the healthcare community. Trauma-informed care, and emergency preparedness programs were not equipped to manage this crisis. There is a multitude of fancy names for professional healthcare-acquired trauma, but a spade is a spade. It's Post Traumatic Stress Disorder. The trauma started with caregiver burnout, workplace violence, and corporate tyranny. The pandemic hammered the final nail in the coffin.

I worked with nursing organizations advocating for changes. More healthcare members came to me with personal stories of suffering. Healthcare workers dreaded admitting their struggles with a mosaic of self-destructive coping mechanisms commonly observed in PTSD victims: substance use, isolation, withdrawal, impulsivity, and aggression. Licensed professionals feared losing their licenses and livelihood. I had been treating nurses, physicians, pharmaceutical associates, and other various healthcare professionals for years. As the pandemic continued to shape the system, healthcare professionals sought me for their patients, friends, and family; they were now desperate to use their personal relationship with me for immediate care. The accessibility struggles my patients endured hit healthcare professionals, and alongside the patients they treated, practitioners suffered like soldiers on a battlefield. Notwithstanding, healthcare professionals, and especially nurses, tenaciously held hope despite the forces that tested their resolve. To be a nurse, Rawsi Williams, BSN would say, "Do what nobody else will do, a way that nobody else can do, in spite of all we go through". The actions of a nurse and the fortitude to remain resilient in crisis exemplifies Hope Advocacy.

Hope Advocacy represents the mechanism required for grassroots movements, epic changes, and revolutions required to cure broken systems. Patients would tell me, "You are the first person I've seen in years that actually cares; I don't care where you go, I'll follow you wherever it is." And that is true. Patients drove hours to see me or used telemedicine. During the pandemic, telemedicine was a critical component for me to help my patients. Maybe it was my autism, maybe my knack for noticing patterns, or my attraction to operational efficiency; whatever it was, healthcare technology became a key source of interest to help and protect my patients. I researched technology and eHealth apps with the same autistic fervor I used to investigate health conditions. I delivered hope while navigating a broken system, pulling patients through, even if they had no money to pay me.

Healthcare professionals generally agree they entered healthcare to help people. Interestingly, even "business-people" echo the same. But did they? The pandemic hit and the industry is called out for exactly what it's been since the 1980s. *A Ford Factory Assembly Line.* Healthcare developed into corporatized chaos World Wars. But you know what? Not EVERYONE is out there trying to exploit patients or nurses. The vast majority just lose themselves in the dysfunctional system that is disorganized, confusing, and costly. Overworked practitioners yearn for a healthier life with more time for family, friends, and community. Instead, they navigate a perplexingly complex system, which exploits vulnerable providers and patients within.

Through my own healthcare journey, I collected a multitude of personal healthcare specialists. Patients and I joked we collected more doctors than Pokémon (nerd alert). The shared experience—specialist after specialist, and test after test—just trying to receive a diagnosis encompassing our symptoms, rather than accruing a plethora of unrelated and compartmentalized diagnoses. I could see the costs of healthcare amassing from the lack of a unifying diagnosis.

I like to subscribe to the philosophy of Occam's Razor. The theory posits that "entities should not be multiplied unnecessarily." In other words, the best solution or theory in medicine should be the one that encompasses all symptoms unified under a single working theory rather than a collection of unnecessary diagnoses. Occam's Razor can be applied to most issues in healthcare from operations to systemic failures. Global healthcare trends demand the use of technology, artificial intelligence, and other computerized and automated systems to streamline convoluted system failures; possible improvements in operational efficiency, providing ethical quandaries are considered with implementation.

New systems promise a future where Occam's Razor can be the rule, rather than the exception, in the diagnostic approach. For my patients, the theory of Occam's Razor offered hope that their body was not a complex labyrinth of unrelated health conditions but rather a singular diagnosis achieved through an amalgamated diagnostic lens. My diagnostic lens considered everyone, including myself. I've posted evidence-based practice articles advocating for patients and myself because everyone is a mother, brother, uncle, or someone to somebody.

In my own practice at Holon Inclusive Healthcare, I didn't make money for months. I went through three billing companies in the pandemic and an overabundance of other infrastructure and technology-related issues. I frantically explored the next best healthcare technology trying to create the most efficient healthcare operating system. I refused to let my patients down, even if it meant treating them for free. Ultimately, my personal healthcare campaign resulted in an upward journey for my own health and wellbeing, followed by financial instability, culminating in the closure of my practice, and a divorce. Yet I refused to give up on Hope Advocacy for my community, patients, and my own children. I don't consider it a complete loss, rather a moment in time where the unstable foundation should be toppled and rebuilt.

The past two years have given me insight into my own deficits where I forgot to practice what I preach. I used to tell my patients to focus on themselves, their values, maintain a healthy work-life balance, and set boundaries. Community disintegrated because we are not unified within our own self and minds, or family units, but rather on everyone and everything else. I lost myself in this world too. I've now set my sights on building a stronger foundation focusing on my family and encouraging my patients to rebuild. You can't be the best caretaker if you are not taking care of yourself and those closest to you.

Everyone can be transformational leaders and supporters of Hope Advocacy, to bring the concept of community back into healthcare while developing a less cumbersome system. Ignoring problems won't ignite change. Everyone must band together—CEOs, nurses, physicians, pharmacists, and drug reps. Everyone has a moral and ethical responsibility to ensure our fellow humans have healthcare equality and accessibility.

Healthcare hits restart by exploring healthcare technology while focusing on personalized medicine and community. Artificial intelligence, genomics, chronic care management, personalized and integrative medicine will all form the cornerstone for global healthcare. No matter what your role is in healthcare, we are all part of a global community and patients at some point. As we build a new healthcare foundation, we can all just start by asking ourselves; is this the course of action I would want for myself, or for a family member?

If all of us do just that, I do believe we may find ourselves fixing this system that imploded with the pandemic. I believe many of us have experienced a BROKEN system during this pandemic. We will be able to foster new systems and produce a sustainable healthcare future.

And like a phoenix that rises from the ashes, we too will *Rise with Resilience*!

Dr. Jessica Giddens has a Doctorate of Nursing, is owner and CEO of Holon Inclusive Health System, is an adjunct faculty at Maryville University, and an industry leader in the mental health and neuropsychiatry fields. In addition to being a #NeuroTribe (Asπ) mom, she strives to promote education and research that decreases stigma internationally. Her experience spans medical-psychiatry integration across the lifespan.

She serves as a speaker, consultant, key opinion leader, radio talk show host, national media tour and podcast guest, clinical research author, website contributor, and advisory board member in the areas of neurobiology, neuropathology, leadership, healthcare technology, artificial intelligence integration, psychopharmacology, genomics, epigenetics, and integrative medicine.

She hopes to revolutionize healthcare and along with her passion for neuroscience, continue to inspire others to expand the horizons for psychiatric care globally. Dr. Jessica Giddens-Whelan hopes to be one of the first doctorly prepared nurse practitioners to be accepted as a member of the American College of Neuropsychopharmacology and become an even more influential leader… and marry Neuralink founder, Elon Musk.

www.twitter.com/DrJGiddensRN
www.linkedin.com/in/drjgiddensrn/
www.facebook.com/jessica.ann.giddens.drjgiddensrn
www.hihealthsystem.com

■

Dean Anderson and Ryan Lipscomb

Banded Together

If you have ever been in a school performing ensemble such as band, choir, or orchestra, you probably understand the importance of rehearsing in person. As band directors, we have often said in rehearsals: "practice is what you do at home on your own, rehearsal is what you do at school with the group;" and "practice is where you learn your part, rehearsal is where you learn other people's parts;" and "you have to hear on your own before you can RE-hear." The music education community could never have expected this type of learning environment could be taken away from them.

On Monday, March 16, 2020, schools in Illinois had their last in person learning day before shutting down for the pandemic. Students were told they had to take their instruments home on this day, along with all the music we were preparing for our next concert and spend the next two weeks practicing on their own. At this point in time, it was only supposed to be a two-week shutdown, and teachers all over the state and country were not prepared for what was to come. Those two weeks, extended into four weeks, then again extended to eight weeks, and finally extended to the remainder of the school year. The smiles of "see you in two-weeks," changed with the realization that we were not going to see these students again in-person.

The instant change to remote learning at the end of the 2019-2020 school year, left us scrambling for solutions. The results were, admittedly, make-shift. Fortunately for us, over the summer, administration told us that we would be seeing our students in-person for the upcoming school year.

Our district started in a hybrid setting for the 2020-2021 school year, where we had students with the last name A-K on one day in person, and L-Z on the next day in person and provided remote instruction for the students that were not in person. We also operated with a shortened school day to eliminate the need to have lunch during the school day to avoid mass numbers of unmasked people in one room. But due to the rising number of cases nationally, before we reached Thanksgiving 2020, our school had to make the shift to 100% remote learning. We stayed this way until February 16, 2021, when we returned to the hybrid setting before finally having everyone back on March 1, 2021. Knowing that our initial efforts at remote learning in band were less than ideal, we set out to create a better teaching solution that allowed our students to learn more effectively in the remote setting.

You might wonder, how do band directors teach band remotely? This is a question we were asked several times throughout the pandemic and one we still reflect on to this day. Our response to the question was usually, "when we figure it out, we'll let you know." Even though the thought of teaching remotely again is relatively behind us, it is still a wonder that band programs across the country were able to operate. If you are wondering what teaching band remotely is like, the best way to experience this is by joining a video call with your family and ask everyone to clap on the count of three. Then sit back and listen to the chaos that follows! We were able to have a bit of fun with this effect, when, on one of our student's birthdays, we attempted to have the class sing happy birthday to her. The cacophony that followed was truly breathtaking!

Because of latency and delay of video and audio signals on the internet, it is impossible to effectively rehearse an entire group of students using a video call. Some students also have bandwidth issues where they cannot have their video on without it stuttering the audio. While technology has made incredible advancements in the last decade, we are still very far away from a time where video can be an effective rehearsal tool. You may have seen "virtual concerts" that school groups put together during the pandemic, and some classical music fans may have seen Eric Whitacre's virtual choir. Something non-musicians will not realize, is that there is a lot of behind the scenes work to make this happen. Typically, a performer will have a click track, a metronome run through and earpiece so that only the performer can hear it, that they play along with while recording. Then a video editor will splice all of the individual videos together. It is not likely that these videos are actually happening live and simultaneously. There have been some apps and programs developed over the past few years to create a "virtual rehearsal" environment, but we are very far away from being able to rely on one for daily rehearsals.

Our strategy for teaching remotely was finding a balance of students' social and emotional well-being and giving students a chance to work with their peers and have rehearsal plans that would lead to productivity. To do this, we would start with all our students from one class, for example our 85 person winds class, combined in one zoom session with every student muted. We played through warmups and exercises that we would normally do in person and have students play along with us. After warmups, we split into our audition-based ensembles, which at our school are Concert Band and Symphonic Band, doing more group appropriate exercises and discussing any playing assignments or things coming up. We then put students into breakout rooms with students in their section and left the rest up to our section leaders. In Concert Band, we had five Zoom breakout rooms to accommodate each instrument group (flutes/oboe, clarinets, saxophones, trumpet/horn, low brass). Our student leaders would coordinate having one person turn a metronome on, have their microphone unmuted and playing through a small section of music while everyone else played along muted, and students would take turns playing on their own. This allowed students to feel like they were playing along with others, but it also pushed them to practice and build up confidence to play in front of their peers. Directors would jump from Zoom breakout room to Zoom breakout room, check in on the groups, and see if students had any questions. This portion of the class was very student led. Students also had playing assignments that they would submit, allowing the directors to see how individual students were progressing and offer individual feedback when necessary. We learned the value of being resilient!

During the pandemic, we have learned patience, understanding, and efficiency. Students are constantly being told they are behind by society and are being overwhelmed with work in many of their classes to "catch up." This is not necessarily saying that teachers are giving students more work than they had regularly received before the pandemic. It is difficult for anyone to go from 0-60 with a flip of a switch, especially when students' organizational skills and problem-solving abilities were challenged less during the 2020-2021 school year, due to the lack of in person learning. We found that, at times, it was easy to forget that, for many students, being in band is an outlet for their stress and a source of fun. It can be easy for directors to push too hard and bring students to the brink of breaking. We have tried our best to keep the understanding of what students are going through at the front of our mind and keep things more lighthearted than we were before the pandemic. We have also been forced to rehearse more efficiently because of the limited time we had in class during the 2020-2021 school year. We have also learned the benefits of doing things in small groups rather than large groups and letting student leaders have more responsibility.

The pandemic has been challenging for everyone. We are very proud of everything our students have been able to overcome. Even though our students faced these challenges, they have had the most successful year in our school's history. A real tribute to their capabilities of *Rising with Resilience!* Our marching band swept its first competition and won the award for best percussion, an award they have never received. They became finalists at a Bands of America regional for the first time in school history. They placed first in class 5A at the Illinois State Marching Band Championships and placed 5th in finals at that competition, which the previous highest ranking was 9th. Our winter guard went on to make finals at two Winter Guard International (WGI) regionals, won the silver medal in their regional competition circuit which is the highest they have ever achieved, and made semifinals placing 23rd overall at the WGI World Championships in their first year ever attending. The challenges these students overcame will shape them for the rest of their lives.

Dean Anderson is the Associate Director of Bands and Director of Percussion at Edwardsville High School in Edwardsville, IL. He graduated as Top Music Education Student with a Bachelor of Music Education from McKendree University and is currently working on completing his Masters of Music Education from Eastern Illinois University. Dean grew up in Highland, IL and currently resides in Edwardsville, IL with his wife Kari. Prior to teaching at Edwardsville High School, he was Director of Bands at Lincoln Middle School in Edwardsville, K-12 Music Teacher in Mt. Olive, IL, and K-4 Elementary Music Teacher in Collinsville, IL.

Dean and Kari are diehard St. Louis Blues and Cardinals fans and enjoy going to watch games live or watching both teams from the comfort of their home with their cat, Gloria.

Ryan Lipscomb is the Director of Bands for Edwardsville High School in Edwardsville, IL. Originally from Oklahoma, Ryan taught band in the Ponca City, Oklahoma school district for eight years before moving to Edwardsville. He attended Oklahoma State University and graduated Summa Cum Laude with a Bachelor of Music degree in Music Education. He has also completed his Master of Music degree in wind conducting from The University of Oklahoma.

An avid cook, Ryan enjoys researching new cuisines and recipes to cook for his family. He currently lives in Glen Carbon, Illinois with his wife, Megan, and two sons, Spencer, and Blaine.

■

Dr. Vanessa Loyd, DNP, PhD, RN

BELIEVE

Not everything that is faced can be changed
But nothing can be changed until it is faced.

–James Baldwin

Growing up in the inner city, my family lived at the level of poverty and my youth entailed lots of violence, drugs, and prostitution. I remember my mother shopping at the Payless shoe store, where she could buy her children's shoes because they were 2 for 1. My mother always conserved when buying food as she bought expired bread because the price was much lower than fresh bread. I was sometimes ashamed but always showed that I was appreciative. My mother would often tell me I was different than her other children. As a little girl, I often pondered and dreamed about what I would do when I grew up. I needed to make money and take care of my family. I narrowed it down to possibly becoming a teacher, nurse, or lawyer so I could take care of my family.

As thoughts of becoming a teacher danced in my head, those thoughts soon changed as teachers often went on strike. I knew whatever profession I chose would require me to go to College. Therefore, my focus was to ensure I would get accepted into College. My parents did not have a strong education background, nor did they have the money to fund my education. My mother finished the eleventh grade, and my dad had a third-grade education. As my dream to go to College was at the forefront of my mind, I worked hard in high school, played various sports (volleyball, basketball, and track), and graduated with a GPA of 3.88. However, I never was guided to prepare for the SAT and ACT, so consequently, I received a score of 17. In several attempts to get accepted into College locally, I was aware that my SAT score was not very good, despite my GPA. I rose with resilience and did not give up. Off to College, I was unsure how the bills would get paid. I tried out for the volleyball and basketball teams, receiving scholarships to play. After completing my Associate's and Bachelor's degree in Nursing, I returned home.

I sought employment at several hospitals, and noticeable obstacles were present. I finally landed a job in the ICU as the only black nurse, and thus this is when I first encountered being accepted into nursing. I often would get the most challenging assignments. I did not complain, nor did I appear bothered about my assignments. In addition, I had to face racial remarks from my peers and sometimes the patients. I would be put in charge at different times to appear these unfavorable behaviors were not happening. While I was enduring these adversities, I would reflect that this what my mom meant when she would tell me I was different. Upon deep reflection, I realized I did not need to be treated the way I had been, and I was not growing professionally or personally. So, I quit and decided to do agency nursing. While working for the agencies, I went back to school because my salary was stable and my schedule was flexible. Not to mention, I had gone through a divorce and was a single mother raising a four-year-old while attending and finishing my master's degree in nursing—that took resilience!

The leader in me did not stop at my master's degree but continued to achieve two doctorates, a Ph.D. in Educational Leadership and a DNP in Leadership in Population Health and Healthcare Systems. I have now come full circle—I am a professor at a University, I am a nurse, and I practice nursing as if I am a lawyer—always thinking about providing the best care I can give to each of my patients. Still, today law school is a part of my conversation about things I would want to accomplish. I still remember how my mother often reminded me that I was different from her other children. Never having asked what she meant, it is now too late. My mother passed away seven years ago, and now I am left to wonder.

I must admit the last two years have made me a stronger person and not question the why. In reality, this period was dark. Personally, I suffered the loss of the love of my life. Professionally, I had to pretend I was strong for my students, who were also not adjusting well due to the pandemic. Many days, I found myself staring into the mirror, feeling paralyzed and asking the Lord what I should do next and how I could help my students. Not once thinking about myself and what I needed to do to keep going and get to a place where I could be strong. I, too, was reeling from much discourse in my life at this time. I realized I owed myself some self-care, and I needed to take care of myself in order to be strong to take care of others. I knew I had to change some things in my life. I always knew prayer changes things, so I began leaning on my faith and the power of prayer. I began with the serenity prayer every day. I keep on Rising with Resilience!

God Grant me the serenity to accept the things I cannot change,
Courage to change the things I can, And wisdom to know the difference

–Reinhold Niebuhr

Daily I wake up citing the serenity prayer before getting out of bed, often thinking about when I achieved my second doctoral degree, the doctor of nursing practice, which was like a beacon of light and provided me with much hope. When I was introduced to the audience, the song "Girl on Fire" by Alicia Keys was played on that unforgettable day. That moment gave me so much energy and strength. So, daily reflection on that particular day provides me with the strength I need!

Resilience is not allowing your situation or circumstances to hold you back. Never give up! Never doubt how much you can bear.

Looking to the hills which cometh your help (Psalms 121).

It is believing and imagining you can fly and you can touch the sky. Moreover, with all, I have accomplished and having a birthday on September 11... I believe I now know what my mother meant when she often would tell me I was different.

Dr. Vanessa Loyd, DNP, PhD, RN, is an Associate Teaching Professor and the Dean's Fellow for Diversity, Equity, and Inclusion in the College of Nursing at the University of Missouri, St. Louis. She has over 30-plus years of nursing experience and 18-plus years of academic experience. Dr. Loyd serves as a liaison between the College and local communities on issues of equity and inclusion to enhance the College's presence as a community partner committed to diversity and inclusion. Dr. Loyd was recently awarded the Chancellor's Inaugural Diversity, Equity, and Inclusion Award. She serves on Missouri Nurses Association Board as a Leadership Fellow and serves as the Vice President for the Missouri Chapter of the National Association for Diversity Officers in Higher Education. Dr. Loyd has a strong interest in and has experience addressing Disparities, Social Justice, Inclusion, Equity, and Diversity.

Dr. Loyd has several published articles: Raising Awareness: African American Faculty Perceptions of the Interview Process and Dismantling Structural Racism in Academic Nursing. Practicing Upstream: Raced-Based Trauma Training for Veteran's Health Administration Nurse Practitioners is under review.

loydv@umsl.edu
loydv@sbcglobal.net

I Am Resilient
I will arise from this hardship
Powerful, beautiful, and wise.
I will cast away this unbearable shell
of a person that I have
become because
I know I am capable of more.
I have God's two feet in front of me,
crouched and coaxing me ahead
One steady step at a time.

I will RISE WITH RESILIENCE!

–Dr. Karen Scaglione

Made in the USA
Columbia, SC
02 July 2022

62658571R00076